D0283759

The God We Can Know

Examining what He has disclosed of Himself

NORMAN A. SHIELDS

AMBASSADOR

BELFAST ◆ **GREENVILLE**
NORTHERN IRELAND   SOUTH CAROLINA

The God We Can Know
Copyright © 1997 Norman A Shields

All rights reserved

Scripture taken from the Holy Bible, New International Version
Copyright © 1973, 1978, 1984 by International Bible Society.
Used by permission of International Bible Society.

'NIV' and 'New International Version' are trademarks registered in the United States
Patent and Trademark office by International Bible Society.

ISBN   1 84030 010   8

AMBASSADOR PRODUCTIONS LTD,
Providence House
16 Hillview Avenue,
Belfast, BT5 6JR
Northern Ireland

Emerald House,
1 Chick Springs Road, Suite 206
Greenville,
South Carolina 29609
United States of America

THE GOD WE CAN KNOW

CONTENTS

Introduction   5

1. God's Knowability   11

2. Attributes of God's Being 25

3. Attributes of God's Character   37

4. God's Triune Nature   47

5. God, the Creator   65

6. The Mysteries of God's Providence   77

7. God's Kingly Rule   91

8. God's Fatherhood   107

9. God as Father   123

10. God's Purpose to save   139

11. God and Election to Salvation   151

12. God's Incomparable Grace   163

Now this is eternal life; that they may know you, the only true God, and Jesus Christ whom you have sent

John 17:3

Introduction

The task ahead

In the age of the motor car there are people who seem able to spend time and money driving around town or country without a definite or a worthwhile destination. They just 'go' for the sake of 'going'. They enjoy 'the going'.

Most people go, however, because they have somewhere to go and something to do when they get there. They have a goal, a destination to which they move.

There is a parallel in the study of theology. We can engage in it just for the sake of doing it - for the enjoyment it brings. But we can also, with more profit to ourselves and to others, take it more seriously. We can set ourselves a goal and make every effort to reach it - we can travel to a destination rather than drift without one.

And what will be a proper goal? So far as these studies are concerned it is that we come to Scripture and find in it the truth that will build us up in the things of God. We will seek to identify and to some degree at least elucidate the teachings of the Bible.

If indeed God has revealed himself and his requirements on the pages of Scripture - and he surely has - then careful study of these teachings is surely worthwhile for every Christian. For those who are called to serve the Lord in the instruction of others whether in ministry, mission, local church or para-church context, such a study is a vital necessity.

A DAUNTING TASK

The English word 'Theology' is derived from two Greek words - *theos* meaning God and *logoi* meaning words. Theology is basically 'words about God'. A theology is a body of such words, a doctrinal construction, a presentation of what is believed to be truth about God.

Often in practice the word theology is given a wider meaning covering the whole body of revealed truth - God's words about himself and about all that he has created. This means that the study of theology is a very demanding and, in some ways, a very daunting task. There is a vast amount of material to be examined and evaluated. There are historical and cultural factors to be grasped because they are essential to an understanding of the teaching.

Theological enquiry is not for the faint-hearted. It is the task of a life-time and even then the servant of God has to admit that there are heights he has not scaled and depths he has not plumbed. To this task we must bring our very best endeavour. Mind and heart must unite in a determined desire to tease out the various strands of teaching and to build up a picture - a sensible systematised picture - of what God says to us in His word.

There are, of course, different theologies. This is because Scripture has to be interpreted and men with their finite and fallen natures understand what it says differently. Each serious student of Scripture to some degree produces his or her own theology. Down the centuries there have been many different theologies developed by prominent thinkers and often adhered to by 'schools' of followers. While we will sometimes mention some of these schools they are treated in much more detail in studies dealing with Church History and Historical Theology.

Much of Scripture, even when translated into English, is fairly easy to understand. However some of it is not so and some parts are hard to reconcile with other parts. As we seek to interpret it we must always remember that we are finite and fallen and incapable of properly grasping all that God has said in his word. As Paul put it, 'we know in part,' that is, we only know ultimate truth in a partial way. We must always recognise, therefore, that any interpretation we make may not be fully accurate, and that the views of others may be closer to the truth than our own and, indeed, that there are areas of mystery that are beyond full human comprehension and about which we must not be dogmatic. Sometimes our highest wisdom will be to stand back and admit that our minds are too small and our logic too inadequate for us to cope with the wonders of the divine being and of what he has revealed to us of himself and of his will.

At the same time we need to recognise that it is the prerogative of the Holy Spirit, the one who searches and knows all things, even the deep things of God, to enlighten human minds to the meaning of things divine. Even the great apostle, Paul, had to admit and was indeed glad to admit, that he was dependent on that Spirit - 'we have received ... the Spirit who is from God, that we may understand what God has freely given us' (1 Cor.2:12).

As we shall see, the Holy Spirit inspired men to write what we now call the Bible. He knows and has disclosed the mind of God. Inevitably then he is the best interpreter of what he himself has caused to be written. As a consequence we will not be able rightly to understand the teaching of Scripture unless we possess the Spirit and submit our whole beings to his control, allowing him to direct our thoughts as we read and as we think about what is written. As Paul puts it, 'The man without the Spirit does not accept the things that come from the Spirit of God for they are foolishness to him and he cannot understand them because they are spiritually discerned (1 Cor.2:14).

We must not then approach the Scriptures in a self-confident attitude relying on our own powers of intellect. Rather we must humble ourselves before the Lord and allow him by the Holy Spirit to teach us whatever lessons he would have us learn.

We must remember that God opposes the proud, but gives grace to the humble; that our duty is to submit ourselves to him, to humble ourselves before him so that he may be able to lift us up in knowledge and in whatever other way he deems fit.

A LIMITED BRIEF

These studies will undoubtedly seem to give scant attention to certain areas that may be of great interest to some who may use them. One reason is, of course, that there are limits to what can be covered in the space available. The scope of the Biblical data is so vast that certain aspects of truth have to be treated separately. We could, for example, devote a great deal of time to the way in which Christians and others should approach God - to the devotional life, private and public prayer and worship. We could devote much space to elucidating the teaching of Scripture on personal behaviour, to ethics, but in both cases separate specific studies are needed.

Even more fundamental is the existence of God. This is a matter usually left for philosophers and for Christian apologists as those who defend the faith against unbelief are known. The studies which follow do not enter and do not need to enter that area which is not handled in Scripture itself. The Bible simply builds its teaching on the premise that God existed before and was active in the beginning of all things (Gen. 1:1) and that he still exists and 'rewards those who earnestly seek him' (Heb. 11:6).

Our goal, as has been said, is to examine the teachings of Scripture and to do so on the assumption that faith in God is valid and is the best basis on which to live. Those who may wish to challenge that assumption must study the works of Christian philosophers and apologists.

It is, perhaps, one of the tragedies of our generation that Christian thinkers are over-much concerned with hairsplitting arguments about doctrinal niceties and too few are giving themselves to the great issue of the day - the battle between theism (belief in God) and secularism. Too few are working on the frontier between belief and unbelief and too often the case for the Bible and for Christian standards goes by default. In setting out to examine systematically the doctrines of the Bible we must not forget the need to defend and to affirm faith and to present the Christian claim in ways that will win the minds and the hearts of our compatriots.

STUDY FORMAT

These studies will follow a fairly consistent pattern. Each main section will be preceded by a summary of its contents and followed by a brief list of books or articles for further reading.

Within most sections there are frequent breaks giving Scripture passages under the heading, 'Look up'. Most of the passages will have been mentioned in the text though the references will not usually have been quoted. These are often given in the order in which they occur in the Bible and not in the order in which the points they support occur in the preceding paragraphs. Part of the value of these studies will be in the effort the reader makes to associate the texts appropriately with the points to which they relate.

One exception to this pattern occurs in much of chapter 1, which deals with God's knowability. In that case a number of full quotations with references are included to make for easier reading by those who may be little accustomed to searching the Scriptures for themselves.

Bible quotations, unless otherwise indicated, are from the New International Version (International Bible Society, Hamble House, Meadrow, Godalming, Surrey, GU7 3JX , UK).

1. God's knowability

1. OLD TESTAMENT EVIDENCE

2. NEW TESTAMENT TEACHING

3. ITS THEOLOGICAL BASIS

1. His image in man
2. His self-revelation
   1. *His creative works*
   2. *His image in man*
   3. *His names and titles*
   4. *His works of redemption*
   5. *His regenerating activities*
   6. *His purposes of restoration*
3. His immanence in creation
4. His omniscience

4. ITS LIMITATIONS

1. He cannot be known in full
2. He is not known by all

APPENDIX

God's names and titles

Chapter 1

God's Knowability

In our introduction we noted that Christian theology begins with the belief that God exists and that he is the source of all that is. 'In the beginning God created the heavens and the earth ... the heavens and the earth were completed in all their vast array' (Gen. 1:1, 2:1).

Scripture never departs from this position of faith. It presents, it proclaims a God who exists and demands that men believe in him and obey him, that they form a personal relationship with him as real as that which can obtain between two human beings and in which he knows them and allows them to know him. We therefore begin by thinking about 'the knowability of God'.

The first thing to notice is that our English word 'know' and its derivatives 'knowledge', 'knowability' etc. can be used in two different ways. They can be used of knowing facts - we can know that the Niagara Falls or the Eiffel Tower exist and we can learn many details about both even without seeing them or experiencing them personally. Similarly we can know that people like the Prime Minister or the President of the United States exist and we can learn many facts about their personalities and their respective ways of life. But there is another sense. in which we can 'know', a much more intimate and inter-personal knowledge in which as well as knowing facts about someone we can actually say that we know him or her. We can usually say this of our parents, our spouses, our brothers and sisters, our children and some intimate friends. We can know facts about another person but not 'know' him in this second sense. Similarly we can know facts - true facts - about God and not 'know' him. When the Bible talks, as it often does, of men knowing God it is in this second or fuller sense of knowing not just facts but the person, of knowing him in person.

Those who know God must, of course, first know some fact or facts about him. Anyone who comes to him (to get to know him) must believe (fact No.1) that he exists and (fact No.2) that he rewards those who earnestly seek him (Heb. 11:6). The danger which must be avoided at all costs is that in our study of theology we become content with discovering and knowing facts about him and fail really to know him or to know him better.

OLD TESTAMENT EVIDENCE

As we read the Bible we find again and again that the key factor in the lives of its heroes is that they knew God. Enoch, we are told, 'walked with God' (Gen. 5:22), a statement which implies that he knew God and gave careful attention to pleasing him. Abraham became known as 'the friend of God', a title which surely implies that he knew God in a personal way. Moses had such a close relationship with God that God could say, 'with him I speak face to face, clearly and not in riddles; he sees the form of the Lord' (Num. 12:8). Samuel did not at first recognise the Lord's voice but when he learned to respond submissively - 'speak for your servant is listening' (1Sam. 3:10) - there began an inter-personal communion with God that lasted to the end of his days. Samuel knew his God.

The list could be prolonged indefinitely as we think of men like Elijah and Nathan, David and Solomon, Isaiah and Jeremiah, Ezekiel and Daniel, the apostles and the other great saints of New Testament times. For them the thing that mattered, the only thing that mattered, was that they knew, that they really knew the Lord. Jeremiah (9:23-24) surely gets the true biblical perspective.

'This is what the Lord says;
    "Let not the wise man boast of his wisdom
    or the strong man boast of his strength
    or the rich man boast of his riches.
But let him who boasts boast about this:
    that he understands and knows me, declares the Lord.'

The point is quite clear - men waste their time when they boast of their wisdom or their skills but when they know the Lord then they have something in which they can properly exult, something they can share with the world, not as a matter of glorifying themselves but of identifying themselves with and reproducing God's kindness and justice and righteousness on earth. To know God is to be like him and to behave like him.

NEW TESTAMENT TEACHING

Our Lord stressed the importance of knowing God. In his great high-priestly prayer he equated a knowledge of God with eternal life - 'this is eternal life: that they may know you, the only true God, and Jesus Christ whom you have sent' (John 17:3). Earlier he had assured the disciples that in knowing him they actually did know God - 'if you really knew me, you would know my Father as well. From now on (i.e., knowing me in an intimate way) you do know him and have seen him ... Believe me when I say that I am in the Father and the Father is in me ...' (John 14: 7, 11). Earlier still he had said, 'I know my sheep and my sheep know me' (John 10:14).

The apostles regarded 'knowing God' as the supreme goal for life. Lack of that knowledge is characteristic of unbelievers - 'Formerly' says Paul to the Galatians, 'when you did not know God, you were slaves to those who by nature are not gods' (Gal. 4:8). He even calls the heathen those 'who do not know God' (1 Thess. 4:5). By contrast the Christian is one who does know God and indeed is known by God.. Paul could address the Galatian believers as those who formerly did not know God bur who now knew him or rather were known by God' (Gal. 4:9). The prayers of the apostles recorded in Acts and the epistles show that they so knew God that talking to him was the most natural thing in the world. Their testimony thus agrees with and joins with the rest of Scripture to demonstrate that God can be known, that he is knowable.

ITS THEOLOGIAL BASIS

1. God's image in man

The fact that man has been made in the image of God means that God and man are so constituted that communication between them is possible, so possible indeed that each can know the other. Because God is spirit and personal and man, made in his image, is also spiritual and personal, he and man can come to know each other in a way that would not be possible if one or other were non-personal. That the image of God in man was marred by the Fall does not mean that it is now non-existent - both Paul and James speak of fallen man as made in that image, 'the image of God.' If man in his essential nature was not constituted with powers of thought, feeling and willing such as are part of the spititual and personal nature of God (see Chapter 2, Attributes, Personality) it would not be possible for him to know God.

2. God's self-revelation

The teaching of Scripture is that God graciously and actively moves towards men and establishes a relationship in which he permits them to know him. Scripture asserts that man is by nature a fallen creature, separated from God by his sinfulness and that it is only as a result of God's gracious condescension that man is permitted to know him.

The knowledge of God comes not because man is able to obtain it by his own effort, but because God in grace is pleased to disclose himself and what he requires to men. That he does so is sheer grace on his part. Without revelation we would neither know about him nor be able to know him.

God's revelation of himself comes to us in a variety of ways:-

1) His creative works,

> 'The heavens declare the glory of God,
> the skies proclaim the work of his hands

day after day they pour forth speech;
   night after night they display knowledge.
There is no speech or language
   where their voice is not heard
Their voice goes out into all the earth,
   their words to the ends of the world.

This aspect of divine revelation through the created universe is accessible to all men. As Paul said, God's invisible qualities have always been clearly seen through what he has made, i.e., the created world, and as a result men who reject the light it provides are 'without excuse.'

2) His image in man

The image of God in man means that man himself in some way reveals the nature of God. His personal nature with powers of thinking, feeling and willing tell us something of what God is. His moral nature with the ability to distinguish between right and wrong, good and evil, tell us something about God - he too makes that distinction and judges his creatures accordingly.

3) His names and titles

The names and titles given to God in the Bible are themselves part of the revelation we have been discussing. An overview of these should help us grasp something of the wonder and majesty of the one we worship as God. To avoid disturbing the main argument they are printed in note form with brief explanations as an appendix at the end of this chapter

4. His works of redemption

Redemption becomes necessary when a person or a property comes under alien control or when life is liable to forfeiture. By yielding to sin man placed himself under alien control - he made Satan his father in terms of his behaviour and placed himself under Satan's control. At the same time he became liable to God's wrath and to death, the penalty prescribed for sin. He therefore needed to be redeemed, to be bought back from slavery and delivered from the penalty of death that rested on him.

The Old Testament story is the story of God redeeming his people. The deliverances of Israel, or of Israelites were preparatory to and pictures of the great redemption to be effected later in Christ. And the New Testament tells of the fulfilment as in the fulness of time God sent forth his Son to redeem men. In him, writes the Apostle Paul, we have redemption through his blood.

Look up Isa. 41:14, 49:7; Jer.50:34; Mk. 10:45; Gal. 4:4; Eph. 1:7; 1Pet. 1:18-19.

5. *His regenerating activities*

Sin caused a separation between man and God, and cut man off from living fellowship with him. As a result man has natural, physical and psychical life but not spiritual life. He has no natural one-to-one, person-to-person, communion with God and so can be described as 'spiritually dead' or as Paul put it, 'dead in transgressions and sins'.

God's saving response is to send his Holy Spirit into individual hearts creating new spiritual life and communion with himself, producing the moral and spiritual qualities that are called 'the fruit of the Spirit' and bestowing gifts for the service of God and of the believing community - 'God sent the Spirit of his Son into our hearts, the Spirit who calls out "Abba, Father"'.

Again there was preparation for this work in Old Testament times as the prophets looked forward to a new covenant arrangement in which men would be motivated to walk in God's ways by God's Holy Spirit resident within them. Our Lord spoke of the Spirit's work in terms of 'new birth' and the apostles variously speak of regeneration, of birth from above, of being made alive and of a new creation. The effect is a living union with Christ, and, in him, with God who reveals himself in a new way as 'Father' to the regenerated soul.

Look up Jer. 31:31-34; Ezek. 36:26-27; Joel 2:28-32; Jn. 3:1-15, 7:37-39; Gal. 4:6; Eph. 2:1-10; Tit.3:5.

6. His purposes of restoration

The three aspects of God's saving work which we have just mentioned are, in a very real sense, works of restoration. They truly seek to restore for man the relationship and the privileges that were lost as a result of sin. However, it is clear that even though redemption is a completed work, restoration is not yet complete. There is more to follow.

The Prophets of the Old Testament era predicted a renewed universe from which sin and suffering would be banished. The New Testament presents Calvary as inflicting defeat but not destruction on Satan and the forces of evil. It looks forward to the return of Christ and to the ultimate redemption and restoration of all things. Satan will be banished, evil will be destroyed and there will be new heavens and a new earth.

Look up Isa. 65:17-25; Rom. 8:18-25, 2Pet. 3:13; Eph. 1:9-10; Rev. 21:1-22:5.

In all his works of salvation God acts sovereignly on his own authority and initiative. It is because he is the Sovereign Lord who really rules over all existence that he could first plan, then reveal and finally effect his saving works. It is because he has such sovereignty that final restoration is assured. His plans are not frustrated because it is impossible for one who is God in the absolute sense to fail to achieve his purposes. He cannot but effect the saving acts he has promised to perform.

Look up Josh. 21:45, 23:14; 1Kgs. 8:56; Heb. 6:16-20; 2Pet. 3:19.

3. His immanence in creation

This is the theological way of saying that God has not abandoned his creation but remains present within it. He may be high and holy, sovereign over creation and distinct from it, yet he is near to each one of us, sustaining our lives and ever able to communicate with us. [Immanence comes from a Latin verb 'manere' meaning 'to remain' and is to be distinguished from the word imminence meaning 'impending' or 'close at hand'.]

God is not an absentee landlord or an uncaring manufacturer who forgets about the goods he has made. He is in his world. We do not need to climb up to heaven or descend to hell to find him. As Paul put it, 'he is not far from each one of us for in him we live and move and have our being' (Acts 17:27-28). Because he is near, because he remains in our world and is involved in all our lives, he is accessible to us - he can be known by us.

3. His omniscience

Scripture presents God as omniscient, knowing all that is or can be known. He does not need to learn any facts about the men and women who enter a relationship in which they know him because he already knows all about them and knows them through and through. When we come to know him it is in the context of his already knowing us.

Dr. J.I. Packer points out helpfully that in the last analysis what matters supremely is not the fact that I know God but the larger fact that he knows me. This, he says, echoes Paul's words to the Galatians - now that you 'know God - or rather are known by God'. He goes on, 'This is momentous knowledge. There is unspeakable comfort in knowing that God is constantly taking knowledge of me in love and watching over me for my good. There is tremendous relief in knowing that his love to me is utterly realistic, based at every point on prior knowledge of the worst about me so that no discovery about me ... can quench his determination to bless me. There is great cause for humility in the thought that he sees all the twisted things about me ... more corruption than I see in myself. There is equally great incentive to worship and love God in the thought that for some unfathomable reason he wants me as his friend and desires to be my friend and has given his son to die for me in order to realise this purpose'. (Knowing God, page 41, pbk. ed.)

ITS LIMITATIONS

We have seen that Scripture presents God as truly knowable. We <u>must</u>, however, be careful that we do not overstate the meaning of this. To emphasise the danger we make two points.

1. He cannot be known in full

God is omniscient and has full and perfect knowledge of us. Man is finite and limited in his capacity to know facts and to know persons. His knowledge of God must therefore be incomplete. If men could fully comprehend and know God they too would be omniscient (knowing everything) and would no longer be mere men but equals with God. By the same token he would cease to be unique and thereby cease to be God.

Nonetheless while our knowledge of God is limited it is fully sufficient for our needs. It is incomplete but adequate. It is also the pre-cursor of an even greater knowledge that will be ours when we arrive in the eternal home prepared for those who belong to the Lord. Says Paul, 'Now we see but a poor reflection; then we shall see face to face. Now I know in part; then I shall know fully, even as I am fully known' (1 Cor. 13:12).

2. He is not known by all

The knowledge of God is not universal. Men do not automatically know him. Even among the Israelites of the Old Testament period there were many who did not know God and some who deliberately refused to enter a 'knowing' relationship with him. Thus we read

> 'They proceed from evil to evil
> and they do not know me, says the Lord. ....
> Heaping oppression upon oppression and deceit upon deceit
> They refuse to know me, says the Lord'
>   (Jer. 9:3, 6, RSV.)

In the New Testament Paul refers to the heathen as those 'who do not know God' (1 Thes. 4:5), a statement which strongly asserts that the knowledge of God is not universal. To know God is not man's right, but a privilege bestowed by grace. It was the Lord Jesus who said, 'no one knows the Father except the Son and those to whom the Son chooses to reveal him' (Matt. 11:27). This raises questions which every human being ought to face - 'Does he - Do I - know God?' and if he does not (or I do not) know him, 'how does one come to know him?'

The purpose of these studies is not primarily evangelistic. The promary aim is to help those who have such faith come to a deeper and richer knowledge of the God in whom they believe. Nonetheless we have a responsibility to bear a witness to this faith and as best we can, show our friends and neighbours how they too can come to faith and to the knowledge of him whom to know is life eternal. There is, therefore, a section at the end of the book explaining the way of salvation. It is hoped that this will be of help to anyone who is seeking God's salvation and that such will come to and find the Lord and enter into an experience of knowing God and of knowing sins forgiven and a sure hope of eternal life.

APPENDIX

THE NAMES AND TITLES OF GOD

1. The designation, 'God'

It is important to understand how the word 'God' itself is used.

1. In the Old Testament there are four related Hebrew words

(1) 'El (205 occurrences) means 'mighty one' - it is frequently used of 'powerful ones' other than God, eg, Job 12:19, Pss. 29:1, 74:15, 82:1, 89:6.

(2) 'Elah (c.90 occurrences, mostly in Ezra and Daniel) - it is used of 'an object of worship,'uaully the Lord

(3) 'Eloah (c.55 occurrences, mostly in Job) - it has a similar meaning to 'Elah

(4) 'Elohim (c.2,270 occurrences) This is a plural form basically meaning 'objects of worship'. It is sometimes (240 times) used of pagan gods and of other powerful spirits and even of powerful men - (Gen. 3:5, Ex. 21:6, Pss. 29:1, 82:6 etc.)

Being a plural form 'Elohim is sometimes taken as evidence of the Trinity (cf, 'us' in Genesis 1:16 etc.) or even of polytheism! In fact it is a plural of intensity meaning the ultimate in power or the One in whom all power is concentrated, ie, the Supreme Being, The LORD

2. In the New Testament there is one Greek word, *theos*, (c.1300 occurrences), which is used as the equivalent of *'Elohim* in the Old Testament

2. The Name of Revelation, YHVH or JHVH

This is the name God disclosed to Moses at the burning bush (Ex. 3). In the ancient world such disclosure was an indication of intimacy and of inter-personal commitment.

*The key passage is Exodus 3:14 - 'I am that I am' or 'I am what I will be' The name is a form of the Hebrew verb **haya** ('to be') and seems to mean, 'I am the one that is' or 'the one that always exists' It affirms that he is constant in nature and in character. The English versions usually translate the name as 'the LORD' in capital letters. Hebrew vowels were not written and by supplying them scholars get either Yahweh or Jehovah.*

*The Greek OT (the Septuagint or LXX) and the NT both translated this name into Greek as **'ho kurios'** meaning 'the Lord'.*

3. Other names or designations

1. **Lord or Master** *(Hebrew, Adoni or Adonay) It is often joined with Elohim, as 'God the Lord'*

2. **Father** *(Hebrew 'abh, Greek pater) In the OT 'Father' defines God's relation to Israel (Isa. 63:16 etc.) In the NT it defines God's relation to Christ and to Christians and even to all men (Acts 17:25ff, 1Cor. 8:6 etc.)*

3. **The Lord of Hosts** *(Hebrew, Yahweh Sabaoth) Usually used in the context of Israel's wars, this name points to the fact that the Lord is/was commander of the armies of Israel and of heavenly hosts (1Sam. 17:45, Isa. 6:3 etc.)*

4. **The Ancient of Days** *(Dan. 7:9,13,22 only). This title stresses God's eternity and unchangeability.*

5. **The Lord God of Israel** *(Hebrew, Yahweh Elohe Israel) This title stresses God's covenant relationship with his people (Josh. 24:2, 1Kgs. 1:30 etc.) - he is their God and they are his people.*

6. **The Holy One of Israel** *- This title is much used by Isaiah and focuses on God's character as one 'separate' from all that is debased or defiled (2Kgs. 19:22, Pss. 71:22, 89:18, Isa. 1:4, 5:19, 12:6 etc. etc.)*

4. Compound titles

1. **El-Shaddai** *means 'the Almighty God' (Gen. 28:3, Job 5:17 etc.)*

2. **El-Elyon**, *means 'God Most High' and stresses God's elevated position as sovereign (Deut. 32:8, Ps. 7:17)*

3. **El-Olam** *means 'The everlasting God' (Gen. 21:23)*

4. **Yahveh-Jireh** *(or **Jehovah-Jireh**) means 'The Lord provides' or 'the Lord will provide' (Gen. 22:8,14)*

5. **Yahweh-Nissi (Jehovah-Nissi)** *means 'The Lord is my banner. (Ex. 17:15)*

6. **Yahweh-Shalom (Jehovah-Shalom)** *means 'The Lord is peace' (Jud. 6:24)*

7. **Yahweh-Shammah (Jehovah-Shammah)** *means 'The Lord is there' (Ezek. 48:35)*

8. **Yahweh-Tsidkenu** *(Jehovah-Tsidkenu) means 'The Lord our righteousness' (Jer. 23:6,16)*

2. Attributes of God's Being

(His essential majesty)

1. LIFE
2. SPIRITUALITY
3. PERSONALITY
4. ETERNITY
5. OMNIPOTENCE
6. OMNISCIENCE
7. OMNIPRESENCE
8. IMMUTABILITY
9. INDEPENDENCE

2. Attributes of God's being

An English dictionary will define the word attribute as 'a property, quality or feature belonging to a person or thing.' God's attributes will, then, be the properties, qualities or characteristics that can be attributed to him.

This understanding of the term is acceptable provided we remember that the qualities, the only qualities, that can rightly be attributed to God are those which he himself has been pleased to disclose to us. God's attributes are not mere human inventions. They are not the product of man's projection of what he feels to be ideal qualities and his building up of a picture of what he thinks God might be like. It is rather a matter of receiving and attributing to him what is disclosed in his own self-revelation.

We must, of course, interpret his revelation and as a result Bible students often have their own distinctive understanding of the attributes. Some diversity of opinion about them is, therefore, inevitable.

It must also be remembered, as has been noticed several times already, that finite man, the creature, is incapable of comprehending God, the infinite, the uncreated. Again man is fallen and even his best efforts at understanding and describing the revelation are affected by the damage done by sin. His interpretations cannot therefore be regarded as final and/or beyond correction. Because man in finite and fallen he cannot, he dare not, be absolutely dogmatic about matters that in ultimate terms are too big for him to grasp.

By way of a working definition we can use the following, 'God's attributes are his perfections as revealed in Scripture.'

Much of the revelation of God's nature and, indeed, of his behaviour, occurred in Old Testament times. Because the New Testament often assumes what the Old has taught, many of the passages from which the various attributes of God are derived are found in the Old Testament.

One point which needs emphasis before we actually look at the various attributes is that they belong together. Though we can distinguish them for purposes of thinking about them, we must never separate them. God is always the sum total of them all and more besides. Our minds are too small to be able to grasp and attribute to him all that he is.

In this study we concentrate on those attributes that focus on what God is in his essence or being. Our next study will examine the sttributes that relate to his behaviour and/or his character.

Nine attributes of God's being call for our attention. These are,

LIFE

God is alive - he has life - he is life. He is never presented as an abstract principle or as the vague 'absolute' of some philosophers. Again and again Scripture refers to him as 'the living God', the one who is alive, the one who alone has immortality, who is not subject to death, the one who is and was and is to come, the ever-living and the everlasting God.

Look up Dt. 5:26; Pss. 18:46; 42:2; Jer.10:10; Dan. 6:20,26; Acts 14:15; Rom. 9:26; 2Cor. 3:3; Heb. 3:12, 9:14, 10:31, 12:22; Rev.1:8, 4:9,l0, 5:14, 7:2, 15:7. (cf 1 Tim. 6:16).

Again the Scriptures tell us that God often asserted that he was/is alive - 'As I live ...'

Look up Num. 14:28; Jer. 22:14; Ezek. 5:11,14,16,18,20, 16:48, 17:16,19, 18:3, Zeph. 2:9.

In harmony with this, Biblical characters often introduced statements of moment by a virtual oath in which the life of God was affirmed - 'as the Lord lives ...'

Look up Jud. 8:19; 1Sam. 14:39,45; 2Sam. 2:27, 15:21; 1Kgs. 17:1; 2Chr. 18:13; Jer. 4:2, 12:6; Hos. 4:15.

SPIRITUALITY

The God of the Bible is essentially a spiritual being. Jesus said, 'God is spirit' (John 4:24 - not 'a spirit', AV). God is ultimate spirit, that from which all other spirits, angels and demons as well as men, derive.

That God is essentially spirit means that he does not need a physical body through which to express himself. We could say that he is 'pure spirit' while men are embodied spirits. That God is spirit also means that he is in no way dependent on material things. He is not limited by space or time or any of the factors which dependence on the created universe entail. He can thus be ubiquitous, can know everything and can transcend time (see below, Eternity).

In ancient Israel the spirituality of God was safeguarded by the second commandment. No material representation of God was permitted and the shrines (tabernacle and temple) were without images. Not all Israelites seem to have understood this, however, and there was frequent recourse not just to paganism but to a paganising of the worship of the Lord. Thus Aaron produced a golden bull or calf as an image that was supposed to represent the Lord - 'a festival to the Lord' (Ex. 32:5).

Jeroboam repeated this folly centuries later. Often Baal-type shrines were developed with stone and wooden images representing the Lord and a female consort or consorts. These were always condemned as heinously sinful by those who were true to the LORD. Reformers, like Hezekiah and Josiah, destroyed them but the paganising influence continued and led eventually to the demise of the Northern Kingdom and to the exile of the Jews in Babylon.

Look up John 1:18, 4:24; Rom. 1:20; 1 Tim. 1:17, 6:16.

PERSONALITY

God is a living spirit. He is also a person. By this we mean that he is self-conscious and has powers of thinking (rationality/reason) of feeling (emotion) and of willing (volition) and that his actions are subject to moral evaluation - they can be judged right or wrong, good or bad in a way that is not possible in the case of non-persons.

As the Biblical revelation unfolds we find God constantly coming into relationship with men on terms that only have meaning if he himself is a person. He is conscious of himself and he shows himself possessed of the capacity to think and feel and will. His actions can be and are morally evaluated but, since he is ultimate life and the source of everything, his actions are necessarily always judged right and good.

The Bible often uses what we call anthropomorphic language when it talks about God. By this we mean that it talks about him as if he were a man. It tells us that he loves, is angry, repents, speaks, has eyes and ears and so on. Such language is used because it is the only language we humans know. It is in one sense inadequate but in another it is thoroughly valid because it brings the truth to us in terms we can understand. It is on our wavelength.

29

Look up

> (1) Re **rationality**, the capacity to think - Isa. 55:8-9; Jer. 29:11; Mic. 4:12; 2Tim. 2:19.

> (2) Re **emotion**, the ability to have feelings (love and anger etc.) - Ps. 73:18, Isa. 63:9; Hos. 3:1; Jn . 3:16,36.

> (3) Re **volition**, the ability to exercise the 'will' both in making decisions and in turning them into action - Jer. 18:5-12; Matt. 6:10, 12:50; 18:l4; Jas. 4:15,

> (4) Re **morality**, the rightness or wrongness of actions (God's are always right) - Gen. 18:25, 14 17; Isa. 45:19; Rom. 1:17; 2Tim. 4:18.

ETERNITY

By eternity is meant that God in not in any way limited by time. He is, in fact, outside of and above time, without beginning or end. If he had a beginning in time there would have been someone or something (even if only empty space) before him; if there should be an end to his existence, there would be someone or something after him. In either of these scenarios he would not and could not be God because some other existence is implied and that existence would then have the quality of eternity while God would not have it. It and not he would be God!

In Scripture God is eternal and the material universe represents but a temporary element in his overall role as Creator and Sovereign.

Look up Deut. 33:27; Isa. 57:15; Pss. 90:2, 102:24-27; 1Tim. 1:17; Rev. 1:8, 22:13.

OMNIPOTENCE

Omnipotence is limitless power. To attribute it to God is to assert that he is the ultimate in power. It must be remembered, however, that he only exercises his power in ways that are right, that harmonise with his character. He therefore, cannot lie and he will not tempt anyone to do evil.

As the ultimate power in the universe, God arranged for it to operate on orderly principles. The stars keep their stations, the earth rotates on its axis and around the sun. The seasons come and go and living things have their life-cycles. There is order and not chaos.

At the same time, God who is always presented as outside and above (as well as within) his creation, can override his own laws. He can step into his creation and bring the unusual, the unnatural to pass. He works miracles which always have a moral purpose and are designed to confirm revelation, to make men realise that he is the Lord.

Look up   Job 9:12; Pss 62:11, 115:3, 147:5: Jer. 32:17; Mt. 19:26; (Mk. 10:27; Lk. 18:27), Rom. 1:20; Eph.1:19; Heb. 11:3; Rev. 1:20 etc.

OMNISCIENCE

Omniscience is unlimited knowledge. To say that God is omniscient is to say that he always perfectly knows all that is knowable, all from our point of view that is past, present or future. 'Nothing in all creation in hidden from God's sight. Everything is uncovered and laid bare before the eyes of him to whom we must give account' (Heb. 4:13).

Look up   1Sam. 2:3; 1Kgs. 8:39; Job 21:22; Pss. 44:21,
           94:9,10,11, 139:3-6, 147:4; Isa. 40:14,28, 55:8-9;
           Jer. 20:12; Acts 1:24; 15:8; Rom. 8:27, 11:33

Foreknowledge in an important aspect of God's omniscience. It is the basis of the Bible's predictions about the future. Because God knew the future, he could disclose it or some element of it to his servants as and when he chose to do so. It is also the basis or, indeed, the essence of election to salvation. It in not simply that he knew in advance how men would react to him and then choose to save those he knew would do so favourably. Such a view would seem to make God a respecter of persons, selecting some as more meritorious than others, an idea excluded by a number of Scriptures. It seems rather that foreknowledge is the same as, or at least involves fore-determination.

Again, if God foreknew that some people would respond to the gospel in penitence and faith and knew this before the world began, then, on our categories of thought, it would seen that that response had been fixed before the world began. If it was not fixed it could not have been known in advance. In that event it must have been God who fixed it because no one else existed then to do so. Logic, which may, of course, be in some way defective, seems to force the conclusion that, in the thinking about God we mustn't abstract foreknowledge from foredetermimtion. If God foreknow anything he must in some sense have foredetermined it.

This view of foreknowledge is difficult to harmonise with Scriptures which appear to imply that man's destiny is not fixed but is decided by the way in which he responds to God. The difficulty is, no doubt, caused by our inability to see things as God sees them - we now only in part.

Look up Rom. 8:29; 1Pet. 1:2.

OMNIPRESENCE

'Omnipresence' is ubiquity and means that God is not limited by space, but is present everywhere and always accessible to men. He is never restricted to any one place, never beyond the reach of the soul that seeks him.

Another word - immanence - is sometimes used to convey this idea. It comes into English from a Latin verb meaning *to remain*. Its use asserts that, while God is transcendent and sovereign over his world and as Creator is distinct from it, he *remains* present within it. He is not an absentee king or landlord. He has not abandoned his creation or his creatures.

Animists (worshippers of spirits) sometimes believe in a supreme deity but think that he has abandoned the world and is not at all interested in men. The philosophic view known as 'deism' is similar. The God of the Bible is not such. He is in his world and everywhere in it. He is immanent and omnipresent. ('Immanence' will be treated in more detail in chapter 4, God's Providential Care.)

Look up Ps. 139:7-10; Isa. 57:15; Acts 17:27-28.

IMMUTABILITY

God's immutability is his changelessness. We live in a changing world. Like the hymnwriter, we see 'change and decay' all around us. The great antidote to concern about the changes that take place in the created world is faith in the unchangeableness, the immutability of God. He is unchanging in his nature and in his character. His attributes in their totality remain constant.

To assert that God is unchanging is not, however, to say that he cannot or does not change his plans or his methods of

33

administering them. There are Scriptures which tell us that he responds to men and to what they are or do. 'He rewards those who earnestly seek him.' He imposes threats and bestows promises on men and makes their implementation conditional on the behaviour of those concerned. If they act righteously, he will bless them; if they act wickedly, he will punish them and, if they amend their ways, he will repent or change his mind in relation to the thing he had threatened or promised.

That this is so seems to assume that things are not determined in advance as was suggested earlier when we discussed foreordination. To some it may even suggest that God is subject to real change. It will be wise for us to try to hold these ideas side by side until we can look at them again in another context (chapter 5). We will then discover that they are both valid and therefore, by our logic, paradoxical .

Look up Gen. 6:6; 1Sam. 5:29; Ps. 102:27; Jer. 18:1-12; Joel 2:13; Mal. 3:6; Heb. 1:12,11:6, 13:8; Jas. 1:17.

INDEPENDENCE (Aseity or Freedom)

Men and all other created beings are dependent on God and indeed on one another, but in Scripture we find that God is ruled by his own counsel. He makes his own choices and thus is independent of all other beings and of all things. He is not limited other than by his own character and this seems to mean that he is completely and perfectly free, he has ultimate freedom.

The assertion that God is completely and ultimately free seems to carry with it the implication that he has ultimate authority. Since no-one can limit his freedom, no-one can exercise authority over or beyond him - 'to him .... the only God our Saviour be (belong) glory, majesty, power and authority through Jesus Christ our Lord, before all ages, now and for evermore.'

The ultimacy of God's authority found expression in his kingship over Israel and his sovereignty over the nations. Gideon, it will be remembered, refused to accept kingship saying, 'I will not rule over you ... The Lord will rule over you.' Subsequent Israelite kings were not regarded as absolute monarchs but as under-shepherds or vassal kings. Foreign nations also came under his sovereign judgment. Our Lord's teaching on 'the Kingdom of God' also points to the sovereign rule of God and to his ultimate authority over all creation.

Look up Jud. 8:22; Pss. 10:16, 24:7,9, 44:4, 47:7, 89:18, 145:1; Isa. 13-21, 23; Jer. 46-51; Matt. 28:18; Luke 12:5; Acts 1:7; Eph. 1:5,11; 1Tim. 1:17; Jude 25; Rev. 17:4.

3 Attributes of God's Character

(His behavioural or ethical majesty)

1. HOLINESS
2. TRUTHFULNESS
3. WISDOM
4. RIGHTEOUSNESS
5. JUSTICE
6. LOVE
7. GOODNESS

3. Attributes of God's behaviour

Some of the qualities which Scripture attributes to God relate to his behaviour and are therefore designated as his ethical or moral attributes. Put together they add up to his ultimate moral perfection.

HOLINESS

The word 'holy' has to do with the separation of someone or something from common usage or availability and his or its separation to a particular role or function. In the ancient Israelite tabernacle vessels were set apart for use in the service of the Lord. Aaron and his sons were set apart to serve an priests. In each case what was set apart was regarded as 'holy unto the Lord'.

The same idea appears in the Israelite view of betrothal. A betrothed girl or fellow was separated from or set apart from those available for marriage and was consecrated or sanctified to one particular person whom he or she would later marry.

Our English words separation, consecration, sanctification and even dedication are often used as synonyms for holiness. To be holy is to be separated to, to be consecrated to, to be sanctified or dedicated to the Lord. Those who are such are called 'saints' or 'those who are sanctified' etc. Used of God the word 'holiness' is an umbrella term which covers his total perfection, his separateness from all that in imperfect, impure, unrighteous or evil. Scripture again and again and again affirms God's perfection in terms of holiness.

Isaiah is the supreme prophet of God's holiness. One of his favourite titles for God is 'the holy one of Israel' which occurs twenty-nine times in the book that bears his name. His vision (chapter 6) of God throned in holiness will have played a part in giving him this all-pervading interest.

In the New Testament holiness is ascribed to all three persons of the trinity (we assume the doctrine of the trinity at this point). Jesus addressed the Father as 'holy Father.' Peter proclaimed Jesus as God's 'holy servant Jesus' and the Spirit of God is consistently called 'the Holy Spirit'.

The holiness of God is always the basis of the Judaeo-Christian ethic. Men are told to be holy because he is holy. Philosophers seek in vain for a satisfactory basis of authority which will keep men and women on the straight and narrow pathway. The Bible vests that authority in God, who is himself perfect in holiness and who presents his own standard of behaviour as the model to which men are to conform.

Look up Ex. 15:11; Lev. 11:44; Pss. 30:4, 89:18, 97:12, 99:9; Isa. 1:4, 5:19, 6:13; 10:17, 29:19,23, 40:25, 41:14, 43:3, 49:7; Jer. 50:29; Ezek. 39:7; Hos. 11:9; Hab. 1:12; Lk. 1:40; Jn. 14:26, 17:11; Acts 4;30; 1Pet. 1:15; 1Jn. 2:20.

2. TRUTHFULNESS

Truthfulness is the total absence of contradiction. What is said or done accords perfectly with reality. Human beings are full of contradictions! They say things that are not in harmony with their actions and they do things that belie their words.

God is different. He is absolutely truthful and is himself the truth. As such, God in absolutely righteous - He cannot act other than consistently - 'God is light (truth); in him there is no darkness (unrighteousness) at all'. (See also Righteousness, below).

One of the main ways in which this attribute is disclosed is in God's faithfulness to his own promises. The religion of the Bible is, in fact, a religion of covenant, a religion that rests on solemn divine promises. To these promises God remains absolutely loyal. The Hebrew word for loyalty to covenant promises is *hesed* but, unfortunately, the AV and the NIV usually translate it as 'mercy'. The RSV renders it 'stedfast love' which indicates something of its force. 'Covenant loyalty' would be an even better translation.

The point is that God is loyal to his covenant because in himself he is truthful, trustworthy and reliable. He is the faithful God, a title given to him on a number of occasions in the New Testament.

Look up Num. 23:18-19; Dt.7:9; Pss. 36:5, 40:10, 89:1-2, 92:1-
      2, 119:90; Isa. 25:1; Lam.3:23; 1Cor. 1:9; 10:13;
      1Thes. 5:24; 2Thes.3:3; 2Tim. 2:13; Heb. 6:18; 1Pet.
      4:19; 1Jn. 5:20.

3. WISDOM

Wisdom is the proper use of knowledge. Knowledge can be possessed but not used. It can be possessed and misused. The God who knows all is one who uses his knowledge in his own and his creatures best interests. In Paul's words he is 'the only wise God.' God's wisdom is seen in his works, in the creation of the universe, in the history of nations and in the insights he gives his creatures about the world and its capacity to produce food and other essentials. His wisdom is supremely displayed in his works of redemption, in the planning and execution of man's salvation. He is, indeed, the source of all true wisdom.

In Proverbs 8 'wisdom' is personified and speaks in a way that seems to indicate a close identification with God himself. Some see this personnification as expressing the character and the role of the second person of the Trinity but this can neithere be proved or disproved. What does emerge later on is that the wisdom which belongs to God was manifest in Jesus, whom God, as Paul says, has made to be 'our wisdom'

Look up Ps. 104:24; Isa. 28:23-26, 31:3; Jer. 10:12; Rom. 16:27; 1Cor. 1:20-25, 30; Eph.1:9, 3:10; Jas. 1:5.

4. RIGHTEOUSNESS

When we say that God is righteous, we are saying that all he does is right. We are not, of course, comparing his behaviour with some standard of rightness outside of himself. Rather the standard is within himself and to this he is always true. Righteousness thus links up with and overlaps truthfulness.

From the earliest times to the end of the apostolic era the righteousness of God is affirmed. There is no contradiction between what he does and what he is - 'He is the righteous Lord.'

Look up Gen. 18:25; Job 36:3; Isa. 45:24; Jer. 9:24, 12:1; Hos. 14:9; Ezr. 9:1; Pss. 19:8, 116:5, 119:138, 129:4; Mt. 6:33; Jn. 17:25; Rom. 1:17, 3:5,21, 6:13, 10:3; 2Cor. 3:9, 5:21; 2Tim. 4:8; Heb. 6:10.

JUSTICE

Justice is that aspect of righteous behaviour which gives proper recognition and fair play to others. In Scripture it is always closely linked with righteousness, the same Hebrew and Greek words serving, in fact, for both ideas. Justice is righteousness in action giving men their due and proper deserts. It involves -

41

1. Punishment of sinners for their sin

That aspect of God's character that reacts against sin and which punishes those who perpetrate it is called 'wrath'. The word wrath often antagonises modern minds but it is clearly present in the divine revelation and must not be ignored. The fact that God is just, and always acts righteously must surely require that he punish those who offend him. Not to do so would be to discriminate against those who please him.

Look up Ex. 34:7; Nah. 1:3,6; Mt. 24:4-46; Mk. 9:41-49; Lk. 21:22-24; Rom.1:18, 2:5, 5:19 etc. 1Thes. 1:10; Rev. 6:16, 16:5-7,19, 19:1-2.

2. Salvation for the oppressed

God's righteousness is his saving action. It may include the punishment of oppressors in order to bring deliverance to their victims. He brings men his righteousness and his salvation.

Look up Isa. 45:13,21-24, 46:12-13, 51:15, 56:l.

3. Justification for the believing

The justifying (declaring righteous) of sinners is an expression of God's justice. He prescribed death as the penalty for sin but he also longed to save the sinner. So in infinite love he bore the penalty himself in Christ so that the demands of his own justice were met and justification could be offered to the sinner. He is at one at the same time, 'just and the one who justifies the man who has faith in Jesus.'

Look up (and read carefully) Romans 3:21-5:11.

4. Reward for the faithful

While salvation is not a reward for merit but a gift of divine grace, there are Scriptures which clearly point to divine rewards for those who faithfully seek and serve him.

Look up Mt. 10:41-42, 25:31-46; Acts 10:4; Heb. 6:10, 11:6; 2Tim.4:8.

6. LOVE

'God is love' - So wrote the apostle John. His words give expression to a truth of revelation that is found all through the Bible. God's choice, for example, of Abraham and his descendants to be his own people was not on the basis of numerical or moral superiority but of his caring concern, his love.

Look up Dt. 7:8, 33:3; 2Chr. 2:11, 9:8; Ps. 47:4; Isa. 43:4, 48:14, 63:4; Hos. 3:1, 11:4; Zeph. 3:17; 1Jn. 4:8,16.

God's love is demonstrated in his loyalty to the covenant promises he made to Abraham and to later Israelite leaders. The Hebrew word 'hesed' emphasises commitment to and fidelity in a covenant relationship. Applied to God it focuses on the fact that, when he sets his love on a person or on people and determines to 'bless them, he will loyally keep his word and will not let them down. He does not and he will not break covenant.

Look up Ex. 34:6; Isa. 63:7; Jer. 32:18 and references to 'hesed' cited above under the attribute 'Truthfulness'.

The New Testament carries the picture forward and makes the love of God a major theme. It uses a distinctive group of Greek words - the noun *'agapé'* (love) and the verb *'agapaõ'* (to love). These words rarely occur in secular Greek writings and highlight the way in which the God of the Bible and the qualities of life he seeks in his people transcend anything found in the paganism of ancient Greece.

Love in the New Testament (in man as well as in God) involves <u>caring concern</u> for another person, a concern that not merely wishes the other well but that resorts to 'caring action' to ensure his or her well-being. God is love in this sense. He showed and ever shows a deep concern for the good of his creatures and he constantly acts for their well-being.

Look up Jn. 3:16; Rom. 5:9, 8:32; Tit. 3:4; 1Jn. 3:1, 3:16, 4:8,16-19 etc.

Love is a comprehensive attribute. The God who is love is full of grace. He is kind in his disposition towards his creatures and is ever ready to bestow on them benefits they do not deserve. He is merciful to sinful men, holding back punishments they deserve and granting them forgiveness when they become penitent before him. It was for mercy that David cried to God when deeply convicted of his sin. It was on the ground of God's great mercy that Daniel prayed that God would forgive his people and restore their city and their sanctuary. In our Lord's parable contrasting the proud self-righteous Pharisee with a despised tax-collector, the prayer of the latter - 'God have mercy on me, a sinner' - took full cognisance of God's disposition to be merciful as well as the man's desperate need for that mercy.

God's love is supremely manifest in the sending of the Lord Jesus to be our Saviour. - 'God so loved the world that he gave his one and only Son ... ' The salvation effected by Christ is entirely the product of God's love. That love moved the Son of God to lay down his life as an atoning sacrifice for his friends. In so doing he took in his own person the penalty due to us for our sin and as a result those who believe in him are justified freely by his grace. Through that same love the believer has new life. He is regenerated and this and every other aspect of salvation springs from the grace of God - as Paul says, 'it is by grace you have been saved'.

When attributed to God, love, like holiness, is an umbrella term that covers a number of aspects of his attitude towards and his care for men and women. Indeed the link with holiness is so clear that we can use the hyphenated term 'holy-love' to summarise God's moral attributes.

Look up Ps. 51:1; Lam. 3:22; Dan. 9:17-18; Lk. 18:13; Jn. 3:16, 15:13; Rom. 3:24, 5:8; Eph. 2:4,5; Tit. 2:11, 3:5; 1Jn. 4:10.

7. GOODNESS

We see goodness as the opposite of badness or evil. Goodness in God and, indeed, in men is an extra quality of supreme worth. It is that something which gives ultimate depth and distinction to all the divine attributes. God is life; he is personal and spiritual; he is unlimited as to time and power, as to knowledge and space; he is unchanging and ever free; he is truthful, wise and righteous. But these are all qualities that could be cold and unattractive to men. The great thing, however, is that pervading all of these attributes of God is goodness. Our God is not a cold abstraction, however great, not the 'wholly other' who (or which) draws little or no response from his creatures. Rather he is personal, warm hearted, loving *and good*. He is absolutely good. All that he is and all that he does are pervaded by his goodness.

Look up Gen. 1:4,10 etc.; 1Kgs. 8:56; Pss .86:5, 106:1, 107:1, 118:1, 119:39,67-68; Mk. 10:18; Phil. 1:6; Heb. 6:5, 12:10; Jas. 1:17.

Goodness sits at the apex of God's attributes. A well-known hymn extols that goodness:-

> 'How GOOD is the God we adore
>   our faithful unchangeable friend
> His love is as great an his power
>   and knows neither measure nor end'.

4. God's Triune Nature

1. OLD TESTAMENT FORESHADOWINGS

    1. Passages implying plurality in the Godhead

    2. The Angel of the Lord

    3. A Divine Son?

2. NEW TESTAMENT AFFIRMATIONS

    1. The Deity of the Father

    2. The Deity of the Son

        1. He presented himself as the Son of God

        2. He exercis ed the prerogative of deity

        3. He sought and accepted faith and worship

        4. He was attested as Son by God himself

        5. He was attested as Son by observers

        6. He was proclaimed as Lord in the epistles

        7. He is presented as eternally God's Son

    3. The Deity of the Holy Spirit

    4. The Personality of the Spirit

    5. The Relationships between the Persons

        1. Father and Son

        2. The Spirit and the Father and the Son

3. THE DIFFICULTIES OF DEFINITION

Chapter 4

God's Triune Nature

The word 'Trinity' does not actually occur in Scripture but the reality to which it refers most certainly does.

'Trinity' is an amalgamation of 'tri' and 'unity' and means 'three in one'. Its use in theology is an attempt to put a name on the fact that, while Scripture ascribes deity to three persons, it yet asserts that there is but one God.

Again we need to remind ourselves that the Supreme Being, God the Lord, is beyond man's full comprehension. Deep mystery will remain until we know as we are known. Nonetheless enough has been revealed to assure us that God is one and that He is three, that he is not one person alone and not three persons each separated from the other, that he is three in one - the Triune God. This is the doctrine of the Trinity.

1. OLD TESTAMENT FORESHADOWINGS

The Trinity is a New Testament doctrine but there are pointers and foreshadowings in the Old Testament, which form an important backcloth to the doctrine itself.

1. Implied plurality in the Godhead

In the Old Testament *'Elohim* is the Hebrew word most frequently used to refer to God. It is a plural form stressing power and sometimes used of heavenly beings or of men who are in positions of power. In that event it is always followed by a plural form verb. When, however, it occurs as the subject of a sentence in which it refers to God, it is always followed by a singular verb. The best explanation of these quirks of grammar is that *'Elohim* is a plural of intensity and indicates that in God there is the supreme concentration of power. He is the ultimate in power, the Almighty.

Nonetheless *'elohim* does sometimes attract to itself plural pronouns and these are often regarded as suggesting some form of plurality, - 'Let us make man in our image, in our likeness' - 'Come let us go down ... ' and 'Who will go for us?'

A further indication of possible plurality arises from the many references to the divine spirit acting with some measure of distinct identity. In Genesis 1:1-2 while God is credited with creating the heavens and the earth it is affirmed that the Spirit of God hovered over the waters. While this and many similar passages do not explicitly teach a trinitarian view of the Holy Spirit, they are harmonious with such a view.

Look up Gen. 1:26, 11:7; Nah. 9:20.; Ps. 51:1, 143:10; Isa. 6:8, 42:1, 48:16, 63:10.

2. The Angel of the Lord

In a number of passages that special angel of revelation, *the* Angel of the Lord, appears. Some Bible scholars are of the opinion that this angel was a second divine person (probably the Son, possibly the Spirit) appearing among men. Certainly those who met this angel often felt that they were meeting with God, but it does not seem possible to prove conclusively that the angel was a divine person.

Look up Gen. 16:7-13, 31:11-13; Ex. 3:2-4 etc.

3. A Divine Son?

The reference to a divine son in Psalm 2 verse 7 - 'He said to me, "You are my Son ..."' - is often taken as pointing to the incarnate Christ. A question mark has been placed after the word Son in the title above because it is doubtful if the Psalmist was thinking in messianic terms. More probably he was reciting God's appointment of himself to kingship and saying that he was appointed to act as a son in relation to the Lord. In that event the son in the psalm cannot be understood as referring to Christ or as an Old Testament indication of plurality in the Godhead. Nonetheless the king can be regarded *as a type* of the Son to come. This enabled the writer to the Hebrews to apply the type to the great King, the truly divine Son, who came as the Christ, the Son of the living God.

Two of the many Old Testament predictions of a Messianic deliverer and ruler involve ascription of deity to the expected Messiah. The first is Isaiah 7 verse 14, 'the virgin will be with child and will give birth to a son and will call him Immanuel'. In the original context there seems to be a reference to a child that would be and was born in Isaiah's day and that was a very clear sign from God to the stubborn King Ahaz. The New Testament clearly declares, however, that the more ultimate fulfilment of the prediction came with the birth of Jesus. He, as none other, was, 'God with us'.

The second passage is in Isaiah 9 verse 6, where the prediction again focuses on the name to be given to a child,

> 'And he will be called,
> Wonderful Counsellor, Mighty God.
> Everlasting Father, Prince of Peace'.

This passage is not actually cited in the New Testament but echoes of its emphasis do occur. Our Lord was indeed the supreme Counsellor. The Holy Spirit was to come as 'another' counsellor, that is, as one who would counsel in the same way as Jesus had done.

Look -up Ps. 2:7 (with Heb. 1:5); Isa. 7:10-17 (with Mt. 1:22-23), 9:1-7.

It is relatively easy for us to recognise in these passages some indication of the trinitarian nature of the Godhead because we read them through New Testament spectacles. From the point of view of the Old Testament writers and of those for whom they wrote - men who did not have the New Testament - trinitarianism is far from clear and Jewish expositors still insist very strongly that there is no such doctrine in the Old Testament.

2. NEW TESTAMENT AFFIRMATIONS

In the New Testament facets of truth additional to those of the Old Testament emerge. They provide the data on which the doctrine of the Trinity is built. The evidence focuses on the ascriptions of deity and of distinct personality to the Father, to the Son and to the Holy Spirit. Each is presented as divine and yet as distinct from the other two. Each is a person; each has a divine nature. They are three yet one, the Triune God, a Trinity.

1. The Deity of the Father

In the Old Testament the word 'Father' was sometimes used to refer to God particularly in his relationship to his people Israel. He was Father, Creator and Lord.

Look up Deut. 32:6; Isa. 63:16, 64:8; Jer. 3:4, Mal. 1:6, 2:10.

Our Lord and the apostles who followed him clearly accepted and built their teaching on the Old Testament concept of God. Other than in completely pagan environments like Lystra or Athens, the attributes of Deity did not have to be supported by argument. The God we meet in the New Testament is thus one and the same as the God we meet in the Old Testament.

The Lord Jesus presented God as uniquely his Father and himself as uniquely God's son. Frequently he addressed God as

51

Father. He spoke of 'my Father and your Father', making a distinction between his own relationship with God and that of his disciples to God. That by Father he meant 'God' is clear from statements like, 'I praise you, Father, Lord of heaven and earth.'

The Apostles similarly used the word 'Father' to refer to God. Peter preaching on the Day of Pentecost spoke of Christ as exalted at the right hand of God and as having received from the Father (i.e., from God) the promised Holy Spirit...' Paul again and again identified one he called Father with God, the Lord. The same is true of the writings of James, Peter, John and Jude.

Look up Mt. 11:25; Lk. 10;21; Jn. 6:27, 20;17; Acts 2:33, Rom. 1:7; 1Cor. l:3; Gal. 1:1; Eph. 1:2,3,l7, 5:20, 6:23; Phil. 1:2, 2:11; Col. 1:2, 3:17; Jas. 3:9; 1Pet. 1:3; 2Pet. 1:17; 3 Jn. 3; Jude 11; Rev. 1:6.

Clearly, then, the New Testament presents the one it calls Father as divine in nature, as the ultimate and unchanging source of all life. The Father is God; he in the creator and life-giver. He is God the redeemer, the one who sent his own Son to save his sinful creatures. Uniquely he is the Father of the Lord Jesus to whom he spoke in terms that he never used of men or angels, for example, 'You are my Son, today I have begotten you' and 'I will be his Father, and he will be my Son'

Look up 1Cor. 8:6; Eph. 3:15; Gal. 1:3,4; Heb. 1:5,7; Jas. 1:17,18.

2. The Deity of the Son

Volume upon volume has been written about the person of the Lord Jesus Christ. The subject is of such importance that a separate and much more extended treatment than is possible here is essential. What is said here is but a brief summary of the main indications of our Lord's deity.

1. He presented himself as the Son of God

That he thought of himself as God's son first emerged when he was taken to the Temple at the age of twelve - 'I had to be in my Father's house' or, as the AV has it, 'about my Father's business.' His awareness of a special and very intimate relationship to God is shown by his frequent use of the word 'Father' and by some statements like those in John which distinguish his own sonship from that of his disciples.

In John's Gospel this awareness also comes through in statements Jesus made about having a heavenly origin and a heavenly destination. His claim greatly angered his Jewish hearers who took it as an assertion of equality with God, something he did not deny but rather confirmed, 'I and the Father are one'.

Look up   Mt. 11:27; 24:36; 26:39, 15:13, 16:17, 18:10,
            14,19,35; 24:36, 25:34; 26:39,53;   Lk. 2:49,
            22:23,29,34,46,   24:49;   Jn.   3:13;   6:33-62,
            8:23,42,58. 14 - 17 (where Jesus refers to God as
            Father on almost fifty occasions). 20:17.

In addition it should be noticed that Jesus accepted and used the title 'Son of God'. In most instances, however, he seems to have preferred, 'the Son of Man', which seems to have had the same force and to stress not so much his humanity as his supernaturalness as the inheritor of an eternal kingdom.

Look up Jn. 3:13; 5:24-27, 9:35, 10:22-39, 11:4; Lk. 22:70-71.

2. He exercised the prerogatives of deity

While on earth the Lord Jesus acted in ways that rightfully belong to God and not to men. He had powers which transcended those of men. He effected miracles, mighty deeds

53

that were signs bearing witness to his divine identity. He healed diseases, turned water into wine, calmed storms, made minute quantities of food adequate for thousands. He knew the inner thoughts of men. He was a teacher the like of whom had never been seen before. He was even able to pronounce the forgiveness of sins. Supremely he rose from death and in resurrection conquered death, man's last and ultimate enemy.

He was different from other workers of miracles in that he could act spontaneously. Elijah had raised the dead but only as a prayerful servant of God. Jesus, in contrast, spoke commandingly. The powers he used were his own. He was, he must have been divine.

Look up Acts 2:14-36, (NB v.36, The one who effected signs and wonders is Lord), Rom. 1:4.

3. He sought and accepted faith and worship

On a number of occasions Jesus presented himself as one in whom religious faith was to be reposed and as the one through whom men must come to God. When such faith was exercised he accepted it and the worship that accompanied or arose from it. He did not rebuke those concerned as the apostles did later on. He was worthy of worship because he was God but they, as mere men, were not worthy of it.

Look up Mt. 10:32,37, 11:25-30, 14:33, 15:25; Mk. 10:17-31; Jn. 6:29, 8:24,28, 9:35,38, 14:1, 20:28,

4. He was attested as Son by God himself

The announcements of his coming given by angels to both Joseph and Mary declared the involvement, the unique involvement of the Holy Spirit in his conception and birth. Mary was told that he would be called 'the Son of the Most High.' The subsequent announcement to the shepherds and the great divine assertions at his baptism and transfiguration make the point that God recognised Jesus as uniquely his son.

Look up Lk. 1:32, 2:11; Mt. 3:17; Mk. 9:7, Jn. 12:28.

5. *He was attested as Son by observers*

The evangelists who wrote of him and some of the people whose words they quote make strong statements affirming his deity.

Look up Mt. 14:33, 16:16; Mk. 1:1; Jn. 1:34,49, 11:27, 20:31; (NB Jn. 1:1-18).

6. *He was proclaimed as Lord by the apostles*

In the early preaching (Acts 1-12) the Lordship of the risen Jesus was affirmed. In the epistles the title 'Lord' (Greek, Kurios), used of Yahweh/Jehovah in the Greek Old Testament (the Septuagint) and in the New Testament is freely applied to Jesus, now risen and exalted at God's right hand.

Of special importance is the application to Christ of Old Testament Scriptures which speak of God, the Lord God of Israel. Examples are Romans 10:9-13 citing Joel 2:32 and Philippians 2:9-11 citing Isaiah 45:23. The implication seems to be that what the prophets spoke or wrote of God the Lord could now be applied with complete integrity to Jesus. The appropriation of such Scriptures could only be valid if Christ was understood to be fully divine.

Look up Acts 2;36; Rom. 10:9-13; 1Cor. 1:2, 8:6, 10:21; Phil. 2:9-11; cf Rom. 1:4, 8:3, 9:5; Gal. 2:20; Tit. 2:13; Heb. 1:1-9.

7. *He is presented as eternally God's Son*

The prologue to John's gospel begins with an assertion that someone called 'the Word' (Greek, Logos) was with God in the very beginning and was, in fact, God's agent in the creation of all that is. John says, 'the Word was God' (not 'a god' as the Jehovah's Witnesses teach). He was divine and was such both in the beginning and when by becoming incarnate he made God known - 'God the only Son, who is at the Father's side, has made him known'.

Jesus himself claimed to exist before Abraham and at the end of the Book of Revelation appropriated to himself words used earlier in that book to assert the eternity of God - 'I am the Alpha and the Omega, the first and the last, the beginning and the end.' The implication of this is that the Son like the Father is eternal and so is the possessor of one of the fundamental attributes of deity. He is God.

Look up Jn. 1:1-5,9-18; Rev. 1:8, 22:13.

Clearly then the New Testament teaches the deity not just of the Father but of a second distinct person, the one who came to earth and was known as Jesus, who died and rose and ascended to heaven as 'Lord and Christ'.

3. The Deity of the Holy Spirit

In the Old Testament the Spirit of God is often mentioned. The Spirit was active in God's creative works and in particular in that operation of God which resulted in man being what he is, a living soul. As the story unfolds the 'Spirit' appears again and again as an expression of God's presence on earth and as doing things that were clearly the works of God.

The Spirit of God bestowed gifts and skills on those whom God called into service and was specially concerned with stimulating good behaviour among God's people.

Look up Jud. 6:34, 11:29; Neh. 9:20, Isa. 61:1-4; Mic. 3:8; Ps. 143:10; Eze. 36:27.

Clearly then the Old Testament writers recognised that, when the Spirit worked, God was at work. However, there is no conclusive proof of belief in the personality of the Spirit in Old Testament times.

In the three Synoptic Gospels this Old Testament presentation seems to be continued. The Spirit was God at work in the life and ministry of Jesus and in the lives of his disciples. The Spirit descended on Jesus at his baptism and led him into the wilderness to be tempted. Jesus claimed to work by the Spirit's power and encouraged his disciples to rely on words the Spirit would teach them. In the great commission he instructed them to baptise new disciples into the name (singular) of the Father and of the Son and of the Holy Spirit. This is usually understood as meaning that the one great divine name (Yahweh/Jehovah) embraces three distinct persons, all of whom are divine. In that event it is a clear assertion of the deity of the Spirit.

Look up Mt. 3:11,16, 4:1, 10:20, 12:28, 28:19; Lk. 4:18-21.

In the Acts of the Apostles we have the story of how the Risen Christ continued his work through the Holy Spirit. The coming of the Spirit at Pentecost and on subsequent occasions meant an enduement of divine power for the disciples.

The Deity of the Spirit is very clearly affirmed in the Ananias and Sapphira incident. Peter accused Ananias of lying to the Holy Spirit and then, referring to precisely the same offence, said that they had lied 'not to men but to God' In other words to lie to the Holy Spirit is to lie to God. The Spirit is thus presented as divine, as possessed of deity.

Look up Acts 1:8, 2:1-4, 4:8ff; 5:3,4, 8:29,39, 13:1-4, 16:1-10.

The deity of the Spirit seems to be a fundamental assumption of those who wrote the New Testament Epistles. When they refer to the Spirit they mean us to understand that the Spirit was a divine person actually present and at work. They connect the Spirit very closely with both the Father and the Son. He is the Spirit or the Holy Spirit of God and He is the Spirit of Jesus or of Christ. He is associated with both in Paul's great appeal for Christian unity and in the bestowal of gifts on believers.

Look up Acts 16:6-7; Rom. 8:15:16; 1Cor. 2:11, 6:11, 12:4-6; 13:14; Eph. 4:3-6; Phil. 1:19; 2Thess. 2:13; Tit. 3:4-6; 1Pet. 1:2,11, 4:14; Jude 20,21.

There is, then, abundant evidence to support the belief that the Holy Spirit is a distinct divine person.

4. The Personality of the Spirit

It is relatively easy to acknowledge the personality of Jesus. In the case of the Spirit the presentation in the Old Testament and in the Synoptic Gospels is not such as demands us to believe in a personality distinct from that of God. The Spirit could be simply the active force of God.

It is in John's Gospel that the distinct personal identity of the Spirit becomes clear. Our Lord is recorded as promising that the Spirit of Truth or 'the Counsellor' (AV, 'the Comforter', Greek, *parakletos*) would come to the disciples after his own departure from them. He refers to the Counsellor as a person. The rules of Greek grammar are actually overridden so that the neuter word 'spirit' (pneuma) in replaced not by the normal neuter pronoun, 'it', but by a masculine one. 'he'.

Clearly, then, our Lord presented the Holy Spirit as a person and since, as we have seen, he was always regarded as divine, we can conclude that he taught that the Spirit is a distinct personal being possessed of real deity - the third person of the eternal Godhead.

Look up Jn. 14:15-31, 15:26-27, 16:5-15; 1Jn. 5:7.

In the New Testament Epistles the personality of the Holy Spirit is again clear. The Spirit can be grieved. The Spirit bestows gifts. The Spirit has a mind and knows God's mind. The Spirit loves, prays and teaches. All of these are activities of a person and witness to the personality of the Spirit.

Look up Rom. 8:26, 15:30; 1Cor. 2:11,13, 12:4-11; Eph. 4:30.

The conclusion that the Spirit is a distinct divine person is supported by the assertion that he is eternal and by the fact that he, like the Son, is associated with the Father in the work of creation. He too has the divine attribute of eternity. He is essentially divine.

Look up Gen. 1:2; Ps. 33:6; Heb. 9:14

5. The Relationships between the three Persons

Scripture has taught us that three persons each distinct from the other are credited with deity. Yet it also teaches that there is but one God - 'the Lord our God, the Lord is one' - He tolerates no rival - 'You shall have no other gods before (or beside) me' is the first commandment. Indeed he asserts that whatever gods men worship or think they worship, there is no god beside or in addition to himself. He alone is God and there is no other.

Look up Deut. 4:35, 6:4; 1Kgs. 8:60; Isa. 44:6, 45:5-6.

There is one God yet there are three persons to each of whom deity is credited. What, we must ask, are the relationships between the persons by virtue of which they can be three and yet one?

Again we need to remind ourselves that we are dealing with matters far beyond our full understanding - 'we know', and only know, 'in part'. Our knowledge depends on the divine self-revelation given us in Scripture and while we make every effort to comprehend that revelation we must avoid any temptation to speculate beyond it.

Another danger arises from the use of human language for divine and eternal realities. The categories of earth are the categories we understand, but in using them of God there is always the possibility that we think of him in earthly rather than heavenly terms and as a result think of him as a super-man rather than as God. Our error will then be like that mentioned in Psalm 50 verse 21 - thinking that God is altogether like ourselves.

1. Father and Son

In human thought fatherhood and sonship belong together and express a very close parent-child or child-parent relationship of interdependence. No-one can be a father without offspring. No-one can be a son without having a father. Sonship implies a beginning in time and a pre-existing father.

We have already seen that eternity is attributed to both the Father and the Son. The Father did not and could not, therefore, have existed before the Son. This being the case, the relationship between these two persons must in some way be different from a parent-child relationship such as we know on earth.

Theologians speak of the Father 'eternally begetting' the Son and of the Son as 'eternally generated' by the Father. But the introduction of the adverb, *eternally*' creates statements that seem self-contradictory and that are certainly paradoxical. Begetting and generating are actions that take place in and are limited by time, while what is eternal is absolutely unlimited by time.

Paradoxical or not some such definition of the relationship seems essential. We must not think of the Son as originating within time because in that event he would be a mere creature and not God. To safeguard this position it seems essential to define the relationship as being without beginning and without end and therefore to speak of the begetting or generation of the Son as eternal.

2. The Spirit and the Father and the Son

Again it seems essential to preserve the full deity of the Spirit and to do this the word 'eternal' has to be used. Theologians therefore link it to the idea that the Spirit proceeds from the Father (John 15:26) and speak of the 'eternal procession' of the Spirit.

The procession of the Spirit is demanded by the very name he bears, the Holy Spirit. The name means the 'one breathed' or 'out-breathed'. After his resurrection Jesus met with his disciples and 'breathed on them and said, "Receive the Holy Spirit"'. Thus the Spirit is presented not just as proceeding from God the Father but as in some way coming also from Jesus. Indeed he himself said he would send the Counsellor, the Spirit of Truth, to his disciples.

The early Christian creeds spoke of the Spirit as proceeding from the Father but later the definition was expanded by the addition of the words 'and from the Son' (one word, *'filioque'*, in Latin). This became a very contentious issue between the Western and Eastern branches of Christendom (the filioque controversy) and was a big factor in what became known an the Great Schism - the division between Rome and Constantinople or between Catholicism and Eastern Orthodoxy, which persists to the present day.

For our present purposes the thing that matters is that our Lord himself clearly taught that he and the Father both sustain a relationship to the Spirit, who is, as we have seen, both the Spirit of God and the Spirit of Jesus. The best way to express the relationship seems to be in terms of 'the eternal procession of the Spirit from the Father and from the Son'.

3. THE DIFFICULTIES OF DEFINITION

The cumulative effect of the evidences we have considered is that in the Godhead we have three distinguishable persons who are yet one in essential nature. The Trinity involves three persons who are not independent but interdependent, who are one in will as well as in essence, one God who subsists as three distinct but not independent persons.

The most famous definition ever produced is probably that emanating from the Council of Nicea in 325. The overall thrust was to defend the deity of Christ against the teachings of Arius who maintained that he was a created being. It includes the following,

> 'We believe in one God, the Father all-sovereign, maker of all things visible and invisible ... And in one Lord Jesus Christ, the Son of God, begotten from the Father as only Son, that is from the being of the Father. God from God, Light from Light, true God from true God, begotten, not made, of one substance with the Father ... And in the Holy Spirit.'

This statement carefully preserves the unity of God and the full deity of the Son. He derives 'from the being of the Father' and from no other source. He is truly God and shares one substance with the Father. What has to be remembered is that, when we are speaking of God, the word 'substance' (Greek, *ousia,* being) refers to a spiritual reality and not to a material one. It was only in His incarnation that the Son took a material body. In His essential eternal being He, like the Father and the Holy Spirit is spirit.

The Creed drawn up at Nicea did not, however, major on the position of the Spirit because that was not an issue in the dispute between Arius and those opposed to his views.

Another famous definition occurs in The Westminster Confession of Faith of 1647. It said,

> 'In the unity of the Godhead there be three persons, of one substance, power and eternity: God the Father, God the Son and God the Holy Ghost. The Father is of none, neither begotten nor proceeding; the Son is eternally

begotten of the Father; the Holy Ghost eternally proceeding from the Father and the Son'.

This definition is obviously more comprehensive and seeks to give a balanced summary of the various strands of teaching in the Bible.

Valuable as these definitions are, they do not exhaust the wonders of the deity and they may, in fact, reflect a good deal of our basic finitude and fallibility. To speak of the Trinity is to refer to the Godhead, to God 'infinite, eternal and unchanging' in all his attributes, one who cannot be likened to anyone or to anything on earth! The word 'trinity' is the best term that has been devised to indicate the reality of one God subsisting as three persons.

5 God, the Creator

CREATION, A BASIC CHRISTIAN TENET

1. A deliberate act of God

2. 'Out of nothing'

3. For the honour of the Creator

4. Effected by the Triune God

GOD'S RELATIONSHIP TO CREATION

1. Transcendent over it

2. Immanent within it

3. Transcendence and immanence in balance

4. Sustaining and providing for it

   1. General Providence

   2. Special Providence

5 God, the Creator

As soon as we open the Bible we find God presented as Creator - 'In the beginning God created the heavens and the earth.' Genesis chapter 1 expounds those words and declares God responsible for the existence of the entire universe with all its material and living parts. The story climaxes with the creation of man, which is considerably expanded 'in chapter 2.

CREATION, A BASIC TENET OF FAITH

The creatorhood of God is maintained throughout Scripture. It is never the subject of argument or proof but is always something believed and affirmed. God is Creator.

The assertion that God created everything, like the assertion that he exists is, and always must remain, a matter of faith. While men have produced theories they thought would prove God's existence or his creatorhood, the Bible itself never attempts such a task. Rather it presents him as active in creation and in sustaining, preserving and redeeming what he has created.

Modern thought tends to deny the idea of creation. It is held to be unacceptable because incapable of logical or scientific proof. It is held to be inconsistent with the theory of and the evidences interpreted as proving evolution. Again the biblical approach is not that of science or philosophy. It is rather to proclaim God as creator and to call on men to believe on him. It has more a doctrine of 'the Creator' than a doctrine of 'Creation'. Its emphasis is that faith in him is essential - 'anyone who comes to him must believe that he exists and that he rewards those who diligently seek him.'

Look up   Gen. 1:1,26-31,5:1-2; 6:7; Deut. 4:32; Neh.9:6; Pss. 65:5-7, 89:11-12, 148:5; Isa. 40:26, 41:20, 42:5, 45:12; Amos 4:13; Mal. 2:10; Mk. 13:19; Eph. 3:9; Col. 1:16; Heb. 11:6; Rev. 4:11, 10:6.

1. A deliberate act of God

The universe is no accident. It did not suddenly appear without cause or plan. Scripture teaches us that God takes careful thought over all his works and effects what he plans. This being so, the idea that things happened or continue to happen by blind fate is ruled out. At the same time what we know of God's character assures us that all that is and, indeed, all that he plans is the work of one who is not just almighty but loving, kind and good.

Look up Isa. 45:10; Rom. 8:29-30; Eph. 1:11; Rev. 4:11.

2. 'Out of nothing' (ex nihilo)

It is usual to speak of God as creating the world - the universe indeed - out of nothing. The point is that God and God alone is, as we noticed when examining his attributes, eternal. He must therefore have existed before anything else, i.e., before the material universe came into being. To allow that before creating the universe, anything at all existed is to accord to that something the quality of eternity and thus to vest it with deity and, in effect, to deny that the Lord alone is God. Creation 'out of nothing' is fully in harmony with Scripture.

> 'Before the mountains were born
> > or you brought forth the earth and the world
> > from everlasting to everlasting you are God'.

Look up Ex. 20:11; Neh.9:6; Pss.33:6,9, 90:2; Jn. 17:24; Eph.
1:4; Heb. 11:3.

3. For the honour of the Creator

Scripture sometimes asserts this as a fact - 'the heavens declare
(do declare) the glory of God'. At other times it demands that
every created being give God the honour due to him as Creator.
Even the heathen are told to sing to the honour of God's name.

Look up Pss. 19:1, 66:1-2; Rom. 11:36; cf. Rev. 4:11 (AV).

4. Effected by the Triune God

We recall the reference to the Spirit hovering over the waters at
the very beginning of Genesis and the use of the plural pronoun
'us' in connection with the creation of man. This, we noted, is
not a proof of the plurality of persons in the Godhead but,
nonetheless, can be taken as a pointer in that direction. In
addition there are a number of statements which associate the
Son or the Spirit with the work of creation.

Look up Gen. 1:2.26; Job 33:4; Jn. 1:3; Eph. 3:9; Col. 1:16;
Heb. 1:2.

GOD'S RELATIONSHIP TO CREATION

As we read the Scriptures we find that in relation to creation
God operates at two levels. Firstly he is distinct from and
outside of it and is sovereign over it. Secondly he remains
within it and so is immediately present everywhere and
instantly responsive to every situation.

It is usual to discuss these two levels of God's relationship to
creation in terms of his '*transcendence*' and his '*immanence*'.
As we will see presently, it is always important to think of him
as both *transcendent over* and *immanent within* creation.

1. Transcendent over it

That which 'transcends' is that which is above something else either in terms of physical or of moral excellence. Mount Everest and the Himalayas in general transcend the mountains of Cumbria or Snowdonia. They are many times as high and cover a much larger area. The President of the United States transcends in terms of power the ruler of small states like Liechtenstein or Swaziland. The life of Jesus transcends every other human life in terms of purity and love and total goodness.

When we affirm the transcendence of God, we are referring to his supreme eminence; we are saying that he is ultimate in the glory and holiness of his person, above and over all creation. We are also saying that he is infinite in authority and has a legitimate right to rule over his creatures and to call to account those to whom he has given commands and the freedom to be obedient or disobedient to those commands. At the same time we assert his independence from creation. He could and once did exist without it and without his human creatures. He is self-existent, self-sufficient and self-sustaining. The world and the men upon it are dependent on him and under his kingly rule, but he himself is dependent on no-one, simply because there is no-one and nothing beyond him. He is absolutely transcendent, the majestic sovereign king of creation.

Look up Ex.-15:18; 1Kgs.8:37; Pss.90:2; 93:1, 96:10, 115:3; Isa. 40:12-28, 42:5; Jer. 10:12-16, 32:17-19; Hab. 2:20-3:15; Mt. 19:26; Lk. 1:37; Acts 17:24, 27-28; Rom. 1:20; Rev. 19:6,

2. Immanent within it

In a brief earlier reference to immanence it was explained that the word derives from a Latin verb meaning to remain and is to be distinguished from 'imminence', which has a different root and a different meaning. It was further indicated that immanence conveys much the same idea as 'omnipresence'.

When we affirm the immanence of God we refer to the fact that, transcendent as he is, he also remains within his creation. It could not exist apart from him. He holds things together, he maintains every form of life - vegetable, animal and human. As Paul said, 'in him we live and move and have our being'. At the same time he is present everywhere and in every situation. He is always accessible to his creatures, none of whom can ever get away from his presence.

God's kingly rule is exercised through his presence in the world as well as from his throne beyond it. General and special providence, including his saving activities, which we have yet to consider, bear witness to his continuing presence in the world. So too does the fact that his ears are attentive to the cries of the righteous and the fact that men can come to know him. He is not far away, inaccessible and uncaring, but near at hand, exercising his control from within as well as from without.

Israel had, of course, a special sense of God's presence and relied heavily on it - 'the Lord Almighty is with us, the God of Jacob is our refuge.' The Christian is even more strongly assured that, wherever he happens to be or to go, the risen Christ - a real divine presence - will be with him 'I will be with you always, to the very end of the age.' He knows that neither height nor depth nor anything else in creation can separate him from the love of God. He is assured of God's loving presence.

Immanence, made more real in Christ and by the Holy Spirit, gives real warmth to our view of God and offsets any tendency to think of him as distant or coldly legalistic. He is the King who knows and understands our needs, our problems and our sorrows and who rules with loving kindness and grace.

Look up Pss. 23:1-6, 46:1-11, 75:3, 139:7-10,18; Jer. 23:23-24; Mt. 13:20, 28:20; Rom. 10:6-8.

3. His transcendence and immanence in balance

Transcendence and immanence are essential elements in God's revelation of himself. They must therefore be seen as belonging together and those who preach or teach the doctrines of Scripture must ensure that they maintain the biblical balance and avoid teaching - or even thinking of - the one without the other.

To stress transcendence alone can lead to a form of *deism* - the idea that God made the world but left it to run on its own energy and has no continuing interest in its welfare. On this view the precious truths of divine providence, redemption and regeneration, become irrelevances and so are discounted or abandoned. An unbalanced emphasis on transcendence alone can also lead to a rigidly deterministic view of God. His control can be seen as an absolute determination of what men are and do, rather than the moral government we have seen to be taught in Scripture. Man then becomes the pawn of a fate that cannot be altered and that may or may not be kind.

To stress immanence alone can also lead to dangerous errors. In the first instance it limits God to his creation. He is in creation and pervading it but not outside or above it. It is then difficult or impossible to distinguish him from it. This tends to a pantheism (all creation is god and God is all creation) that is thoroughly foreign to the biblical revelation. Pantheism brings God down to the level of earth and lies behind a great deal of modern thought. Much evolutionary theory, for example, assumes that God, if it allows his existence at all, works from within his universe which is seen as moving or working towards a divinely ordained goal. J.A.T. Robinson and his followers, who maintain that there is no God 'out there' or 'up there' and that God is 'the depth of being', man's own being, seem to operate on the assumption that God is totally immanent and indeed, imprisoned, within creation. The New Age Movement, which is so influential today, is very much built on the pantheism of Hinduism and other eastern religions.

To avoid these errors - and others besides - we must be careful to maintain the biblical stance that God is both transcendent and immanent. The two ideas may seem to some minds to be nearly or even totally irreconcilable but, as so often in theology, truth is not in one extreme or the other and not in a synthesis of the two but in the paradox of both together.

Paul surely got the balance when, preaching to the Greek politicians at Mars Hill, Athens, he said,

> 'The God who made the world and everything in it is the Lord of heaven and earth and does not live in temples built by hands. And he is not served by human hands, as if he needed anything, because he himself gives all men life and breath and everything else. (i.e., he is transcendent) ..... 'he is not far from each one of us. For in him we live and move and have our being... ' (i.e., he is immanent).

While we may not be able to produce a logical explanation of how God can at the same time - and at all times - be both transcendent and immanent - sovereign in majestic otherness and sovereign in glorious nearness - we can accept both positions in faith and we can live in the light of them knowing that he, God the Lord, is not only transcendent and immanent but loving, kind and good. We shall become more aware of his goodness when, later on, we think of his fatherly love. For the moment let the Lord's own words spoken through Isaiah re-iterate the paradox -

> 'For this is what the high and lofty one says ...
> "I live in a high and holy place (transcendence)

but also with him who is contrite and lowly in spirit"' (immanence)

Look up Isa. 57:15, Acts 17:24-28

4. Sustaining and providing for it

The Bible presents the Lord as sustaining everything that he has made. He is not like a manufacturer or a trader who wants only to sell his wares and take no further responsibility for them. He is not like someone producing a machine and leaving it to its own devices or to run down using whatever energy it possesses till that energy is exhausted. Rather he ensures that it holds together and keeps going - 'in him all things hold together' - The Son ... sustains 'all things by his powerful word.' The point surely is that the universe God created is maintained by the very God who created it - the stars keep their station, the earth rotates on its axis and around the sun, the atoms hold together by the sustaining power of God. Because he is creator and sustainer there is continual order in the universe. There is no chaos.

In a special sense God sustains human life. The reproductive processes function as his gift. Once life is given men depend on God for its continuance. Man is indeed a dependent creature - 'in him,' says Paul, ' we live and move and have our being.'

Look up   1 Sam. 1:27; Job 1:21; Pss. 22:9, 65:9-13, 107:23, 104:29; Dan. 5:22; Acts 17:28.

The teaching of Scripture on God's sustaining care is usually thought of in terms of his providence - his provision to sustain the universe in all its parts, mineral, vegetable animal, human and spiritual. The term 'Providence' is rightly used to cover every aspect of God's relationships with creation. Often, however, it is used more narrowly of his care for the human race or, indeed, for those who are God's people. Dr. J.I. Packer cites what he regards as the normal definition of providence in Christian theology - 'the unceasing activity of the Creator, whereby in overflowing bounty and goodwill he upholds his creatures in ordered existence, guides and governs all events, circumstances and free acts of angels and men and directs everything to its appointed goal for his own glory (Art.,Providence, New Bible Dictionary, 1962, p.1050ff and 1996, p979f).

Providence can be recognised as operating at two levels. General Providence is God's care of the entire creation and Special Providence is more specific to individuals or groups and particularly to his own people.

1) General Providence

God provides the air men, animals and plants require for their own survival. He provides food and every other essential for living species. The Psalmist can in eloquent terms praise God as the provider of these necessities:

> 'You open your hand
>   and satisfy the desires of every living thing'

More fully he (or another Psalmist) sings:

> 'He makes springs pour water into the ravines;
>   it flows between the mountains.
> They give water to all the beasts of the field;
>   the wild donkeys quench their thirst.
> The birds of the air nest by the waters;
>   they sing among the branches.
> He waters the mountains from his upper chambers;
>   the earth is satisfied by the fruit of his work.
> He makes grass grow for the cattle,
>   and plants for man to cultivate -
>   bringing forth food from the earth:

> Wine that gladdens the heart of man,
>   oil to make his face shine,
>   and bread that sustains his heart.

The Lord Jesus taught that this providence extends to the whole world. 'He (God) causes his sun to rise on the evil and the good and sends rain on the righteous and the unrighteous.' He cares not just for men but for the birds of the air and the lilies of the field.

Look up   Pss. 36:6c, 104:1-35; 145:9,16; Isa. 40:26; Mt. 5:45, 6:26ff, 10:29; Acts 14:16-17, 17:25-26; Rom. 11:36.

2) Special Providence

There is abundant evidence in Scripture of a more specific side to providence. This involves special acts of God designed to meet the needs of individuals or groups and particularly to care for those who are his own people. Special providence is a very precious reality to believing men and women.

We think, for example, of the way in which God provided a lamb for Abraham to use as a substitute for Isaac or of the way in which he provided food and water and other necessities for the Israelites at the time of the Exodus. We think of the way in which he provided for Elijah in the home of the widow at Zarephath and of the way in which he used Ebed-melech to deliver Jeremiah from death.

Our Lord assured his disciples that God, their heavenly Father knew their needs and could be trusted to meet those needs. Paul gave a similar assurance to the Philippian Christians, 'Do not be anxious about anything ... and my God will meet all your needs according to his glorious riches in Christ Jesus.' Paul himself knew times of need. At one point in his life he was the victim of an unspecified disability, a thorn in his flesh, a messenger of Satan to torment him. Looking back he could see this as a provision with a moral purpose, to keep him humble and to make him more dependent on the grace of God. Through this experience he had learned to delight in provisions that appeared adverse - weaknesses, insults, hardships, persecutions and difficulties - because through these the Lord's power was made perfect in him. The provision of grace was sufficient for his need.

Look up   Gen. 22:8,13; Deut. 2;7; 1Kgs. 17:6-16; Pss. 103'
104, 121:1-8, 139:7-18; Isa. 28:26,29, 41:8-10; Jer. 38:7-13; Mt. 6:24-34; 2Cor.12:7-10; Phil. 4:6,19; 1Tim. 4:16-18; 1Pet. 5:7.

6. The Mysteries of God's Providencee

THE INEQUALITIES AND INJUSTICES OF LIFE

FACTORS CONTRIBUTING TO THE MYSTERIES

1. Human sinfulness

2. God's retributive justice

3. God's testing of faith

FACTORS UNDERPINNING DIVINE PROVIDENCE

1. God's essential goodness

2. God's mysterious ways

Chapter 6

The Mysteries of God's Providence

Throughout history God's providence and, indeed, the whole of his kingly rule over the affairs of the world, have given rise to difficult problems for men and women of faith. These difficulties focus mainly on what are perceived to be inequalities and injustices and on the very existence of evil. Like Job, afflicted by the loss of his family, his farm and his health, men ask why it happens, why, if there is a God who is good, he allows these adversities to happen.

William Cowper, the eighteenth century Christian poet, who suffered from severe bouts of depression, highlighted the mysterious side of divine providence in the opening verse of a well-known hymn,

> God moves in a mysterious way,
>   his wonders to perform;
> He plants his footsteps in the sea
>   and rides upon the storm

THE INEQUALITIES AND INJUSTICES OF LIFE

Scripture recognises that there are people who do not enjoy a providence that meets even their basic needs or that gives them an enjoyable quality of life. There are many records of drought and famine, of greed and crime, of plague and war, of disease and disability resulting in deprivation and death, often on a massive scale.

At a number of points the Old Testament seeks to grapple with the apparent inconsistency between a providence that is believed to be good and an experience that appears anything but good. The people of God were taught that God rewards fidelity to his covenant requirements and punishes, or at least disciplines, those who are unfaithful to those requirements. Their problem was that experience often seemed to be the reverse of this, the righteous suffered adversity while the wicked enjoyed prosperity. It often seemed as if God's providential care was prejudiced and unjust or absent altogether.

In the main the answer of Scripture to this problem is that wrongs will not go unrequited but will be put right either later in this life or in the life to come. Job had deep longings that one day God would vindicate him by putting right the injustices he felt he was suffering. Sometimes despite the darkness of his soul he had flashes of faith and could confidently assert his assurance that eventually his vindicator, his redeemer, would do this for him.

Two psalms, 37 and 73, deal with the same problem. In the first the psalmist addresses those who worry and fret because of the prosperity of the wicked and tells them to wait for the Lord, who will in due course exalt them and cut off the wicked. In the second the Psalmist feels that he has kept himself pure to no purpose because he had problems while the wicked seemed to be totally carefree and to be increasing in wealth. But then he checks himself and says that trying to understand all this and reconcile it with faith became oppressive to him. At least that was the case till he entered the Lord's house and in some way came to understand the final destiny of the wicked - God would bring them to ruin. In effect the inequality and the injustice that troubled his soul would in the end be put right

The New Testament explains the delay in the exercise of God's retribution on the wicked in terms of his great desire that those concerned repent before him. Peter says he is not slow in keeping his promise about the coming again of Christ and the judgment of mankind - 'He is (rather) patient ... not wanting anyone to perish, but everyone to come to repentance.'

Many Christians seem to ignore what appear to be inequalities and injustices in the human condition, especially when they and their immediate family and friends are not the victims. But the problem really does exist and gives rise to doubts and fears in many hearts. They have also been used again and again by those who delight in making sport of Christianity.

For our part we can make no claim to watertight answers that will meet the objections of sceptics or resolve all the uncertainties of the doubter. The most we can do is to try to focus on a number of factors that are, or may be, involved in our human experience of God's providence.

Look up Lev. 26:14-46; Deut. 28:15-68; Job 19:25-27; Pss. 37; 62:11-12; 73; Prov. 24:11-12; Mal. 3:18-4:3; 1K. 13:1-5; Rom. 2:1-11; 12:19; 1Cor. 4:1-5; 2Pet. 3:9.

FACTORS CONTRIBUTING TO THE MYSTERIES

1. Human sinfulness

Sin is always present in human life. It distorts every situation. God appointed man to rule over the rest of his creation but, because of sin, man has failed to be equitable in his treatment of his fellows and of the resources God has provided for them. Man's greed and mismanagement have meant that some people enjoy comfort and ease while others are exploited or deprived. Some communities have been forced to live in areas where the climate and the general environment are unsuitable for the production of food and where there are few, if any, valuable natural resources.

To the extent that man's inhumanity to man has produced want and injury for others, man and not God is to blame for inequality and injustice. Indeed Scripture always holds men accountable for their socially unjust behaviour. Cain was his brother's keeper; Ahab was guilty of dispossessing Naboth from his vineyard and of having him executed on the basis of false witness. The Assyrians were guilty of cruelty and the economic exploitation of nations they had conquered even though at the same time God used them to chastise Judah. Men can never relieve themselves of responsibility for the sufferings they inflict on others by blaming God. They bear and must bear responsibility for what they themselves do. Their sinfulness is undoubtedly a major factor in happenings and conditions that appear to be unkind or unjust providences.

Look up Gen. 4:1-16; 6:5-7; 1Kgs. 21:20-26; Nah. ch.3; Jas. 5:1-6.

The existence in the world of human sin and of moral evil raises serious questions in relation to the providence of God. Difficulty arises as soon as we try to explain how a God who is the only God, who is completely sovereign and who in his own nature is essentially good, so good that he cannot look on evil or tolerate wrong, could ever have permitted sin or moral evil to exist. To explore this difficulty is really to try to push our understanding a step back behind the time-frame of our human existence and into the eternal dimension. In doing so we need to be exceptionally careful that we do not become impertinent before God - like the clay questioning what the potter is doing or the offspring questioning the begetting and bearing roles of its parents.

Look up Hab. 1:12-17; Isa. 45:9-10.

In the Old Testament one Hebrew word, (ra') serves for adversity and for moral evil or sin. Job talked of the Lord visiting him with trouble (ra') where before he had enjoyed

81

good. By this he meant that adversity had come to him in place of the prosperity he had previously known. In Psalm 23 David declares that, because God was with him, he feared no evil, no adversity. Rather God's goodness - the opposite of adversity - would follow him all his days. In both cases the Hebrew word (ra') means trouble, trial or adversity and relates not to immoral behaviour but to circumstances involving opposition, unjust criticism, illness, injury and the like.

Look up Job 2:10; Ps. 23; Jn. 8:44; 1Jn. 3:10; Rev. 12:9.

Our main concern now, however, is with 'evil' in its more sinister sense, of rebellion or sin against God's will and God's laws. Its first manifestation in human life was in the Garden of Eden but clearly it did not originate there but with the Devil who, according to the Apostle John, 'has been sinning from the beginning'. Satan or the Devil leads the whole world astray. He is the father of lies.

Clearly the Bible acknowledges the existence of moral evil. It was because of its existence that God promulgated laws and it effected a work of salvation designed to save men from it and enable them to resist and conquer it, not in their own strength but in his. In our Lord's death and resurrection Satan and the forces of evil he controls were defeated and those who become Christians, who, by faith, are in Christ can live in his victory and with the assurance of ultimate complete deliverance into a realm where evil will have no place whatsoever.

The Bible even speaks of angels that sinned, that did not keep their position and that are bound in everlasting chains for judgment on the great day. Evil thus existed outside the realm of human life and is not just co-terminus with it. Scripture, however, insists that in the end there will be a new earth that will be free from all forms of evil - both adversities or troubles and moral evil. In doing so it indicates that evil is not eternal and is not therefore in essence a second absolute principle or a rival god. Scripture, nonetheless, presents a persistent conflict between good and evil in what we know as time, but there is no eternal dualism - no two gods, one good and one evil. God, the Lord, alone is God and while Satan is sometimes called the god, the powerful influence of this world, he is a god with a small 'g' - never with a capital 'G'.

Look up   1Cor. 15:25; Col. 2:15; Heb. 2:14; 2Pet. 2:4; Jn. 3:8; Jude 6; Rev. 20:7-15; 21:1-22.

The most we can say - indeed the wisest thing we can say - is that the origin of evil is shrouded in mystery. We do not know why a God who is perfect goodness should choose to allow it to originate or to continue in existence. Ultimately, if he alone is God, there seems no way in which, on our categories of logic, the conclusion that he foreknew, permitted and ordained its existence can be avoided. But to state that conclusion does not mean that God can be blamed for the multitude of evil actions performed by his creatures.

Note: The AV of Isaiah 45:7 reads, 'I make peace and create evil' but the NIV, 'I bring prosperity and create disaster' is more accurate because it interprets the Hebrew word, ra', not of moral evil but of physical adversity or disaster. If this is correct, as seems to be the case, this is not a statement in which God accepts responsibility for the existence of moral evil, but an assertion that his providential care includes the judicial disciplinary and training aspects of adversity.

Look up   Isa. 45:7.

2. God's retributive justice

God has built into creation and into human life the capacity to hit back at acts which contravene his laws. If a finger is put in the fire it gets burned and its owner suffers pain and disability. Those who receive toxic substances into their lungs or stomachs pay the price in impaired health and often in shortened lives. Those who commit sin sooner or later reap its wages - it finds them out. Men reap what they sow and God's providence has ordered things to ensure that they do so.

In the second place,God as the Sovereign judge of all <u>continually</u> exercises a moral government over men. He reacts to man's behaviour inflicting punishments and bestowing rewards. He can impose a judicial penalty at any time and, indeed, often did so in Biblical times. David, for example, suffered the loss of the child he had begotten in adultery. The loss was an act of divine retribution which could not be averted even by intensive fasting and pleading with the Lord. So too in New Testament times Ananias and Sapphira suffered divine judgment as a result of their deliberate deceit.

Look up   Num. 32:23; 2Sam. 12:14-18; 2Chron. 18: 27-34; Acts 5:1-11; Gal. 6:7-10.

A note of caution must be sounded at this point. It is that, while what has just been said is true, we must never reverse the line of thought and work from the sufferings and the troubles men endure to the conclusion that God is punishing them for sins they personally have committed. We can in a general way say that sin brings its wages of sorrow and death. We can even say that all suffering results from the sinfulness that invaded human life in the Garden of Eden. However we can not and we must not ever tell anyone who is suffering illness or adversity that his suffering is the result of specific sins he has committed. It may in fact be, or be partly, the result of the person's own sins but no one can be sure that this is the case. No human being therefore has the right to make an accusation - judgment must wait till the Lord comes.

Job's friends tried to explain his suffering in terms of sin and drove him to virtual despair because he knew he had not done the things of which they were accusing him. The real problem was that suffering was being wrongly interpreted as proof of

84

sin. A similar belief can be seen among those who told Jesus of Galileans whose blood Pilate had mixed with sacrifices. They thought that the victims were the worst sinners in Galilee but our Lord said an emphatic 'no' to the idea and repeated his repudiation of it by referring to eighteen men on whom a tower had fallen in Siloam.

Look up Job 4:7-9, 15:2-35: Lk. 13:1-5; cf., Jn. 9:1-3; 1Cor. 4:5.

3) God's testing of his servants

In Job's case there was another element which is material to some of the problems of providence. Job was being tested, though he himself did not know it. The providence that had given him prosperity and happiness was withdrawn and a chain of adversities took its place. From the prologue to the book we know that God permitted or rather instigated the deprivations he suffered. It was God who called Satan's attention to Job and who, in permitting him to act, set limits to how far he could go. Job was greatly pressed and was upset by many doubts by virtue of the false pastoral care he received from his so-called friends. In the end he met God face to face and surrendered himself in brokenness before the Lord. Nonetheless he received no explanation as to why he had been afflicted but, when he was broken in spirit before the Lord, he entered new blessing - 'The Lord blessed the latter part of Job's life more than the first'.

There was also an element of testing in the way God dealt with Paul. The thorn in the flesh given as a messenger of Satan to torment him drove him to his knees and brought him to the brokenness of spirit that accepted it as a providence through which he could experience more of God's grace.

The Authorised Version normally translated Hebrew and Greek words meaning 'test' or 'try', 'testing' or 'trial', by 'tempt' or 'temptation'. This can produce misunderstanding and makes it important that readers of that version carefully investigate the proper meaning of those and related words wherever they occur. For example, God's challenge to Abraham to sacrifice Isaac was a test and not a temptation to do evil - 'God tested Abraham' is the New International Version's rendering. Paul can similarly speak of himself as having served the Lord with humility and tears and of having been severely tested by the plots of the Jews.

When the devil, the tempter, attacked our Lord in the wilderness his motive was to tempt or entice him to do evil. Our Lord was tested in the process and passed the test with flying colours. Satan's aim was, of course, to damage Christ and to undermine God's saving purposes in him. When Jesus taught his disciples to pray 'lead us not into temptation' the petition may include 'testings' within its purview but the contrast in the next line - 'deliver us from the evil one,'strongly suggests that enticement to be and to do evil is in view. Followers of Christ will always need and should always pray for deliverance from such temptation.

Whatever the testings that God ordains or allows for his creatures, He himself does not and will not entice them to do evil. When tempted, no one should say, 'God in tempting me'. For God cannot be tempted by evil nor does he tempt anyone. However, God does test his people and some, perhaps indeed all of the adversities they suffer are likely to involve some element of testing.

Look up Gen. 22:1; Mt. 4:1-11, 6:13; Acts 20:19; 2Cor. 12:7-10; Jas. 1:2-3,12-15.

In so far as adversities - including the inequalities and the injustices we have been considering - are testings ordained by God, they must be seen as part of his 'Special Providence'. Joseph knew that the evil intentions and actions of his brothers, actions that had cost him great suffering, were in fact providential. 'You intended to harm me but God intended it for good to accomplish what is now being done, the saving of many lives'. Similarly Job and, much later on, Paul were severely tested but they were being trained and moulded in holiness by what they suffered.

The Lord Jesus was tested, supremely so, indeed, when he was subjected to the ultimate indignity of being put to death by crucifixion. The antagonism of the Jews, the fact that his disciples deserted and even denied him and the pressure of the divine will that he bear in his body the debt of human sin were tests of incredible magnitude. His death took an extremely cruel form but all was in God's set purpose and foreknowledge and what the Jews did by handing him over to the Romans was at one and the same time an act for which they were responsible and part of God'a providence for Jesus and for the world of men. The tests to which he was subjected are without parallel in all history and the benefits that flow from his resolute acceptance of God's will are equally without parallel - 'He bore our sins in his body on the tree, so that we might die to sins and live for righteousness; by his wounds you have been healed'. Scripture teaches that what we see as adversities are, or often are, gracious provisions of a God who is testing our faith and training us to be more conformed to his own image.

Look up Gen. 50:20; 2Cor. 12:7-11 (again!); Acts 2:23; 1Pet. 2:24-25.

FACTORS UNDERPINNING PROVIDENCE

1. The essential goodness of God

It needs to be remembered that Scripture presents providence as an aspect of the nature and character of the living God, a God who is personal and warm - the God and Father of our Lord

Jesus Christ, the one whose essential character is love. And because God is love his intention is that the ravages of sin in man's life be overcome - that man be redeemed and made fit for fellowship with himself.

Once the absolute goodness of God is accepted it becomes much easier to handle the inequalities and the apparent injustices that come to oneself or to others. The problems are not solved, however, on an intellectual level but in terms of religious experience - a trust in God is developed that enables one to see that behind the stresses and the sufferings there is a God who cares and whose chastenings and testings, however unpleasant, are, in fact, benign providences.

Perhaps the best way to see the goodness of God's care is to examine - or better still experience - the benefits of his saving work in Christ. The man who enjoys forgiveness and knows himself favoured with God's salvation can endorse the words of Paul, 'He who did not spare his own son but gave him up for us all will also along with him graciously give us all things.'

Look up 1Kgs. 8:56; Pss. 107:1, 118:1; Mk. 10:18, Rom. 8:32.

2. God's mysterious ways

Our highest wisdom is to acknowledge that there is an element of mystery attaching to God's providence. It is easy to see God's hand at work in events that turn out to benefit ourselves or some cause we support, but not so easy when his providence seems to work against our cherished dreams or our selfish desires. Often we can see something of his designs when we look back later on, but at the time his providences baffle and disturb us. In such situations the recognition that God works in mysterious ways can be helpful in tiding us over the difficult period when we have to walk totally by faith and without any understanding of what the Lord is doing for our good and for his own glory. The psalmist (Asaph) knew these things and wrote describing how in his own life faith had triumphed over adversity and despair.

> When my heart was grieved
> and my spirit embittered,
> I was senseless and ignorant;
> I was a brute beast before you.
>
> Yet I am always with you:
> you hold my right hand.
> You guide me with your counsel,
> and afterwards you will take me into glory.
> Whom have I in heaven but you?
> And earth has nothing I desire besides you.
> My flesh and my heart fail,
> but God is the strength of my heart
> and my portion for ever

William Cowper again gets the message,

> Judge not the Lord by feeble sense,
> but trust him for his grace;
> Behind a frowning providence
> he hides a smiling face.

Job argued against providence but finally caved in and acknowledged the mystery of God's dealings with him. As he bowed in reverence before the Lord he got no rational explanation of his sufferings but he found peace in a personal relationship with the Lord and in leaving matters in his hands.

God's ways are beyond our comprehension. There is and there always will be mystery. Our place is to walk by faith even when we cannot understand what he is doing.

> For my thoughts are not your thoughts,
> Neither are your ways my ways',
> declares the Lord.
> 'As the heavens are higher than the earth,

So are my ways higher than your ways,
And my thoughts than your thoughts.

Jesus made it absolutely clear that man was not and could not be privy to a full understanding of the mind of God. Certain things were revealed or were being revealed by Jesus himself but others were not to be known or understood even by the disciples. Thus, in relation to his own return in glory, our Lord said, 'No-one knows about that day or hour, not even the angels in heaven, nor the Son but only the Father.' In this matter there was a divine secret and so far as the disciples were concerned the date remained - and remains - a mystery. That this is more generally the case is clear from Paul's words, 'we know in part.' There are and always will be aspects of God's dealings with us that are beyond our - beyond human - ken.

Look up   Job 42:1-6; Ps. 73:21-26; Isa. 55:8-9; Hab. 2:20-3:19; Mt. 24:36; Rom. 8:28-30; 1Cor. 13:9; Phil. 2:12-13.

7. God's Kingly Rule

IN THE WORLD OF NATURE

IN THE HISTORY OF MANKIND

   1. The difficulty of relating Divine sovereignty to human freedom

   2. The problem of God's permissive will

IN THE JUDGMENT OF HIS CREATURES

   1. The continual process of judgment

   2. The prospect of final judgment

   3. The wrath of God

Chapter 7

God's Kingly Rule

'The Lord God Almighty reigns.' The Apostle John heard the heavenly choir sing those words.

God's kingly rule arises from his creatorhood and involves both power and authority. He is all-powerful, omnipotent, and therefore able to control his creation. He is eternal and his priority over creation ensures his authority to rule over it. At the same time, being who he is and what he is, his exercise of sovereignty is an aspect of his providence, of the provision he makes to ensure that his creation functions according to his will and moves in an orderly way towards the ends he desires for it.

Evidence of God's kingship is found throughout Scripture. He rules in the world of nature, in the history of mankind and in the lives of individual human beings.

IN THE WORLD OF NATURE

The natural realm in its entirety is under God's control and its orderly operation bears witness not just to his creatorhood but to his ongoing kingship. Even those who have no knowledge of special revelation can learn of him through observing his works in nature and are without excuse, if they fail to heed the message those works proclaim.

The heavenly bodies - the sun, the moon, the stars and the earth itself - keep their stations at his behest. Here on earth the seasons and the weather are controlled by God. He gives fertility to the land, to the flocks and to the herds. In human life he can give or withhold children and he has power to sustain life or to take it away.

Look up   Gen. 8:22, 16:2a; Job 26:7-14; Pss. 29:1-11, 103:19, 104:10-16, 127:3; Isa. 40:21-26, 44:24-28; Jer. 31:35; Mt. 5:45, 6:28-38; Rom. 1:20.

It has to be recognised that God's control of creation in these general terms is largely a matter of ensuring that there is conformity to patterns built into creation itself. These patterns are usually called 'the laws of nature' (or natural laws), but we must be careful not to allow ourselves to think that such laws are independent of the Creator. The Biblical view is that the patterns by which the created world pursues an orderly rather than a chaotic course are expressions of God's continuing sovereignty over it. He is the ruler, the King of creation.

The Bible also presents God as able, when he so chooses, to super-impose himself on the laws of nature and to transcend or alter them in order to fulfil some purpose of his own. When this happens we have what we call miracles or what Scripture often terms 'signs' or 'wonders'. Miracles seem to have been most numerous in the days of Moses, in those of Elijah and Elisha and at the time of our Lord and his apostles, but they did occur at other times and in principle there seems no good reason for denying that they can still occur. Indeed there is very good reason for believing that they can because to deny the possibility of miracles is really to deny the continuing sovereignty of God. If he were unable to step into his world and override natural laws he would have ceased to be totally free in the exercise of omnipotence and would have ceased to be God.

Look up   Ex. 7-10 (the plagues), 15:11; Josh. 10:12-13; 1Kgs. 17:5-6, 13-16, 17-24, 18:36-39; 2Kgs. 4:1-7; Lk. 7:11-17, 23:45; Jn. 6:5-13, 11:38-44; etc.

IN THE HISTORY OF MANKIND

The clear testimony of the Old and New Testaments is that the Lord is God of all the earth, that his rule extends to every remotest corner inhabited by men. As the psalmist puts it, 'The Lord reigns, let the earth be glad' or again, 'Say among the nations, "The Lord reigns."'

Human history is HIS STORY, the outworking of his sovereign rule in those who acknowledge him and gladly submit to his rule and, indeed, also in those who do not do so. The day will come when every knee will bow to recognise his kingly authority, but meantime even where his rule is not acknowledged it operates. Because the Lord reigns, the proper response of the nations is to tremble before him and to praise his great and awesome name.

The book we know as Genesis portrays God's rule over the men of antedeluvian and patriarchal times. God knew of early man's wickedness and could not ignore it. With grief and pain he responded by decreeing the flood. Centuries later he called Abram, who became known as Abraham, and brought him to Canaan to establish a new race who would be a chosen people through whom he would bless the world. The vicissitudes of Abraham's life and of the lives of his descendants again and again show how God ruled in human affairs. Even what was intended by Joseph's brothers as evil was a providence laid on by God for the good of the entire house of Jacob. Surely God was indeed ruling and he, rather than men, controlled history.

The theme continues right through the Old Testament and into the New. The main emphasis is on God's sovereign rule over those he was pleased to bring into a covenant relationship with himself, first the Israelites and then Christian believers. He preserved Israel in Egypt at a time of considerable oppression. He raised up leaders like Moses and Joshua and a long succession of judges, prophets, kings and sages, whose role was to carry out his purposes in the nation. Then in the fulness of time he raised up Christ to inaugurate the new covenant and to initiate the kingdom of God as a spiritual and moral entity open to men of every tribe and nation. Even those who crucified Jesus acted, we are told, in accordance with God's set purpose and foreknowledge.

Then he exercised his rule in the calling of apostles and others to spread the gospel and extend his kingdom. Their lives clearly followed patterns ordained for them by the Lord. Paul, for example, was miraculously brought to faith and put into the ministry. His missionary travels were under the constant guidance of the Holy Spirit and his sufferings and trials all contributed to the fulfilment of God's purpose for his life.

At the same time God's control of the history of people, who were not in a special covenant relationship with himself is also clear. He inflicted serious diseases on Pharaoh and his household because Sarah had been taken into the palace harem. Even though Abraham had deceived by calling Sarah his sister, God controlled events in Egypt to ensure that Abraham and Sarah were reunited and sent on their way. Clearly too, God was in control when Pharaoh put Joseph in charge of the land of Egypt and so ensured a food supply and a haven for Jacob and his family.

In a similar way God raised up foreign nations, the Midianites, the Assyrians, the Babylonians and others to chastise Israel or Judah. But in so doing he was exercising his kingly rule. This was also the case when he raised up Cyrus, king of Persia, who freed the Jewish captives from exile in Babylon. Though they didn't know it or didn't know the Lord, these people were doing his bidding and, in fact, demonstrate his ultimate authority and his universal rule. He, the Lord, was and is in control of human history.

The fact that God rules in history is also clear from the way in which he enabled some of his servants to predict events before they actually happened. Indeed one mark of a true prophet was that his predictions came true. There are examples like those of Isaiah predicting the advent, first of the Assyrians, then of the Babylonians and finally of Persians led by Cyrus. Jeremiah also predicted the exile in Babylon and actually lived through the trauma of Nebuchadnezzar's seiges. If God's servants could be given accurate advance information on these events, the events must have been in God's plan and must have come about under his rule. Predictive prophecy bears witness to God's kingly rule in human history.

The cumulative effect of these and many complementary records is that the Lord rules over human history. He is indeed King of kings and Lord of lords.

Look up   Gen. 6:5-7, 12:10-20, 41:41-45, 50:20; Pss. 97, 99; Prov. 16:9; 20:4; Isa. 10:5, 45:1-7; Hab. 1:5-11; Dan. 4:3; Acts 2:33, 16:6-7, 21:10-14; 2Cor. 12:7-10.

1. The difficulty of relating divine sovereignty to human freedom

While God works out his sovereign will in human history there is another side to the Biblical picture. This declares that men are not robots or puppets controlled mechanically or magically by an arbitrary despot, but are free and responsible beings, who are held accountable for their actions and who are somehow governed according to those actions.

There is, of course, a problem when we attempt to reconcile divine sovereignty with human freedom. If, on the one hand, God is really sovereign over human life, it seems impossible to assert that man is truly free. Similarly, on the other hand, if man is truly free and able to do his own thing, it seems impossible to believe that God is really sovereign over him.

96

Yet the clear picture is that God is sovereign and that man is a free being who can choose what he will or will not do. Because he is free and his actions are his own, he can be judged on the basis of his behaviour and, indeed, of the inner thoughts and motives that produce his behaviour.

Israel was often permitted to go its own way and it frequently did so. When that happened God's Kingship operated in the application of sanctions. His people were subjected to punishments like plague or drought or invasion and plunder at the hand of foreign powers. These sanctions had the aim of producing repentance and a new submission to God's rule. When the people repented God was pleased and prospered them again. The principles by which he exercised this government over his people are set out clearly in Leviticus 26 and Deuteronomy 28.

Jeremiah's visit to a potter's house showed that the exercise of God's kingly providence was not a matter of arbitrary fate but of moral responsiveness. At the time Judah was under the threat of exile in Babylon and the prophet was to proclaim that, if Judah changed its ways, God would repent of the evil (the exile) he had threatened. Equally, when he promised a people blessing and they turned away from him, he would not fulfil his promise. Bane and blessing are presented as somehow dependent on the moral condition of people. In the immediate situation Judah refused God's call to repentance and the threatened evil soon became a reality as successive hordes of Babylonian soldiers overran the land and took thousands upon thousands of captives back to Babylon.

In similar vein individual kings like Saul, David, Solomon and Uzziah were free to indulge in follies which brought disastrous results in their own lives. Scripture faithfully records God's displeasure and shows that he treated each as a morally responsible being.

The same is true of the New Testament Christian. He is free and responsible for all he does. His life's work will be judged and, if good, will survive like precious stones or precious metals survive fire. If his works are not what God wants they will not survive, but will disappear like wood, hay or stubble do in fire. He himself is in danger of becoming weak, sickly and asleep. Clearly many Christians suffer - and indeed, need to suffer - divine discipline (AV, chastisement) in order to learn not to dishonour the Lord and in order to share in his holiness..

The same principles operated on the wider canvas of the pagan nations . They had freedom but they came under divine scrutiny and their activities were always subject to his judgment. As universal sovereign he pronounced judicial penalties on the nations. Pharaoh's Egypt experienced such penalty through the ten plagues that preceeded the Exodus. The prophets Amos, Isaiah and Jeremiah devote a good deal of space to pronouncements of woe on foreign nations. Isaiah and Habakkuk focus on the divine use of Assyria and Babylon as agents for the chastisement of Judah and in both cases declare that the super-power of the day would be held responsible for its actions and would be punished for its own haughty pride and callous cruelty.

The Lord's kingly rule over men and nations is not then a matter of arbitrary fate but of true morality. God is a moral being, who deals with men as moral beings. He imposes sanctions and tells them clearly what consequences they should expect to flow from the use and from the abuse of their freedom. His rule is based on moral principles and on the response of a moral being to other moral beings.

Look up Lev. 26:3-39; Deut. 28:1-68; Ps. 97; Jer. 18:1-17; Mt. 25:31-46; Rom. 2:5-11, 14:9-10; 1Cor. 3:12-15, 11:30; Heb. 12:4-13.

and with reference to the accountability of the pagan world

Isa. 13:1-20:6, 23:1-18, 46:1-47:15; Amos 1:3-2:3; Obad.; Nah.1-3; Hab.2:2-20; Rom.1:20-32.

2. God's permissive will

Many Christians have what appears to be a neat way of answering the questions people ask about the divine will. They say that God *permits* adversities and evils but does not decree them and is therefore not responsible for them. Such things come, rather, on the initiative of Satan or of malign human desires and are allowed by God under what is termed, 'his permissive will'.

If, as we have maintained, God is sovereign over the whole of creation and is omniscient, knowing all that happens before it happens, does it not follow, we ask, that what he permits he does, in fact, ordain? If he knows certainly that something will happen, then that something must have been fixed for as long as he knew about it and, since his knowledge is eternal, it must have been fixed in eternity. And if it is fixed in advance there can be but one who fixed it, God himself. To allow that some other person or power planned the happening so that it could be known eternally is to make that person or power either equal to or greater than God and to deny God's ultimate position and his ultimate authority. It is to make him less than God.

Such seems to be the logical conclusion flowing from the sovereignty and the omniscience of God but the logic may be defective and lead to a fatalism that is not biblical. Scripture, in fact, presents, as we have seen already, another side to the picture, namely, that in making man in his own image God has given him, permitted him to have, a freedom that somehow reflects his own freedom. God's sovereignty over men is not the rule of fate but, as we have been saying, a moral government that operates through moral precepts and that reacts to the morality of those over whom he rules.

This being the case it seems that we have two options - we can either try to synthesise the two lines of thought or try to hold the two in some sort of balance. If we try to synthesise we will, it seems, tend to one extreme or the other and either fall into the error of fatalism (i.e., God determines everything) or into a view of man's freedom which is equally erroneous and denies God's sovereignty (i.e., God determines nothing). To hold a balance and a more truly Biblical stance, it seems necessary to think of God's will as somehow operating at two levels, first ordaining or decreeing events which surely come to pass and secondly at a distinctly ethical level, telling men what they ought to do but yet permitting them not to do it.

Adam and Eve were created good and were told not to eat certain fruit. That was a moral precept and clearly they-were free to obey or disobey. We cannot say why they chose to be disobedient, but we have to admit that God neither stopped them from doing so nor created them in such a way that they had no choice. In some sense he permitted them to do wrong and therefore permitted all the evil consequences that flowed from what they did - 'sin entered the world through one man and death through sin, and in this way death came to all men, because all sinned'.

To speak of God as permitting things (his permissive will) seems necessary to help us grapple with issues that are really beyond human comprehension. If we could view things from God's perspective, the picture would be different and we would see that there is no conflict between God's sovereignty and man's freedom, and no ultimate distinction between what he decrees and what he permits, but that perspective is not our privilege in this life. We have to remind ourselves again that we see but pale reflections, that we know only in part. We have to confess with Job, 'those (the works of God men see in the created world) are but the outer fringe of his works; how faint the whisper we hear of him!'

Look up Job 26:14,; Rom.5:12

IN THE JUDGMENT OF HIS CREATURES

The fact that God's rule over men is of a moral nature brings into focus the role of God as judge. As sovereign ruler of the created universe he is ultimate in authority and as such is supreme Judge.

To 'judge' is simply to pass an opinion on someone or about something, but in the context of a legal system the word takes on the more specialised meaning of passing a verdict on someone's conformity to or breach of a legal code. Used of God the idea of judgment is conditioned by what we know of his character - he is righteous or just and he is good. His judgments will then be just and good. The judge of all the earth will do right. As Paul said, 'He will judge the world with justice' (in righteousness). The legal code by which he judges is his own law, a transcript of his own character and the very epitomy of righteousness or justice. His omniscience ensures that he is in possession of every possible piece of relevant information and able to make a judgment that truly accords with fact and that is both wise and right.

Look up Gen. 18:25; Acts 14:31; Rom. 3:3-4, 14:10-12; 2Cor. 5:10.

1. The continual process of judgment

From the creation to the ultimate consummation the Lord judges his creatures. Adam and Eve quickly encountered a condemnatory judgment after they ate the forbidden fruit. King Saul encountered divine rejection because of his disobedience. David's adultery with Bathsheba and his murder of her husband likewise called forth God's condemnation. So did the deceit of Ananias and Sapphira and the sins of a host of others.

Equally the loyal devotion and the faithful obedience of Noah, of Abraham and of many others were rewarded. Cornelius 'prayers and gifts to the poor' were acknowledged in heaven. God, says the writer to the Hebrews, 'is not unjust, he will not forget your work and the love you have shown to him as you have helped his people ...'

Some of God's judical acts are applied with a corrective aim and are usually called 'chastisements'. Such discipline, as the writer to the Hebrews says, seems painful rather than pleasant at the time but later it produces a harvest of righteousness. Paul told the Corinthians that he himself had experience of this - he had been given a thorn in the flesh to keep him from becoming conceited. Despite three requests to God for its removal, he had to live with it. Through it he found the fruit of righteousness and learned that God's grace was sufficient for his weakness.

Similarly Israel and the pagan nations around her were constantly under God's scrutiny and received from his hand reward and punishment for their conduct. There is a 'so far and no further' in God's dealings with nations. The Sovereign, who is the Lord, reigns as supreme judge over the entire race, His continual acts of judgment are in fact expressions of his moral government of the world.

Look up Gen. 3:16-19; 6:1-8; 1Sam. 15:16-29; 2Sam. 12:1-14; Prov. 3:13; Acts 5:1-11; 2Cor. 12:7-10; Heb. 6:10, 12:4-13.

2. The prospect of final Judgment

The Old Testament has a number of pointers to an ultimate judgment of all mankind, but it is in the New Testament that the prospect emerges with real clarity.

Some of the Psalms (notably Psalms 37 and 73) grapple with the problems created by the fact that righteous men often suffered adversity, while the wicked prospered - a fact that seemed to call in question the justice of God's providence. The answer given was that such travesties of justice would be short lived and that in the end the wrongs of this life would be put right. Job, beset by a multitude of troubles which he felt were unjust, could look forward to vindication by one he called his redeemer or vindicator.

Our Lord often spoke of an ultimate judgment and indicated that the Father had committed judgment to himself. His famous Olivet discourse presents his return as involving a separation between righteous and unrighteous people, which would settle their destiny and which, therefore, has to be understood as an act of final judgment. He pictured all nations gathered before his throne to be judged and separated as sheep from goats, the sheep to gain eternal life and the goats to endure eternal punishment.

The Apostles in their preaching and writings often stressed the certainty of the final assize. God has fixed a day for it, 'a day of wrath when his righteous judgment will be revealed and he will give to each person according to what he has done'. As sure as man is destined to die, he is destined thereafter to face God's judgment.

Some scholars think that the Scriptures point to a series of separate judgments - for believers, for unbelievers and for nations. Others of equal sincerity find that position unacceptable. What is clear in Scripture is that in the end all men, good and bad, believers and unbelievers, will stand before God and receive his verdict on their lives. God's judgments even extend beyond the human race and embrace the non-corporeal spirit beings we call angels.

Look up   Job 19:25-27; Ps. 37:18-20,38, 73:1-28; Isa. 11:3-9; Dan. 12:2; Mt. 13:30,40-43, 24:29-51, 25:31-46;

Acts 17:31; Rom. 2:5-11; 1Cor. 3:13; Heb. 9:27; Jude 6.

3. The wrath of God

It would be improper to deal with God's position as judge without referring to his anger or wrath. God's wrath is his reaction to sin and evil in his creatures.

The Old Testament refers to God's anger using a number of words which suggest raised emotion. In the New Testament the most common Greek word is *orge* which emphasises not the anger of hot-emotion, but a more deliberate and reflective response that takes account of all the circumstances and imposes a carefully thoughtout penalty.

In God, wrath or anger is always righteous, always rational, always wise, always an expression of his perfection. Nonetheless the picture revealed in Scripture is stern and sombre. God can be angered and man's highest wisdom is to avoid rousing his wrath.

The Old Testament has many references to God's anger and to the offences which evoke it. The worship of idols, the breaking of the Sabbath, the shedding of blood, the breaking of wedlock by adultery, coveteousness and other breaches of the decalogue are prominent. The fullest description of God's wrath is probably that in Nahum 1:2-8, where the apparently harsher aspects are nevertheless balanced by statements like, 'the Lord is slow to anger' (v3) and 'the Lord is good' (v.7).

Similar ideas emerge in the teachings of Jesus who again and again warned of the ultimate danger of incurring the full weight of divine wrath and ending up in the eternal fire prepared for the devil and hie angels. It was Jesus who said that God's wrath rests on those who reject the Son. The apostles continue the emphasis and warn the ungodly of the danger of falling into the hands - the wrathful hands - of the living God.

Wrath is then a clear element in the divine revelation. In ultimate terms it involves the condemnation of the impenitent to complete perdition, to what Jesus called 'eternal punishment'. Men may decry the idea. They can ignore it if they please but, like it or not, they cannot avoid it except by paying heed to God's warnings and by accepting God's provision for their salvation.

One point which must be emphasised is that God's wrath must not be isolated from other elements in his character. Nahum links it with his patience and goodness, Paul links it with his kindness - 'the kindness and sternness of God'. We must be careful lest we tip the balance and so magnify God's wrath that he appears to be a harsh being who is impossible to please. Our God is, of course, a consuming fire. He reacts in wrath against sin but he is also good and kind and merciful. His desire is not to damn but to save and, as we shall see, his love is such that he took the wrath due to men and in the person of Jesus bore it himself.

Look up Nah. 1:2-8; Mt. 25:41; Mk. 9:48; Jn. 3:36; Rom. 1:18, 2:5, 11:22; 1Thes. 1:8-9; Rev. 6:16-17, 14:9-11, 16:19; cf. Rom.2:4; 1Tim. 2:4; 2Pet. 3:9.

8 God's Fatherhood

OLD TESTAMENT PRESENTATION

    God, the Father of a covenant people

OUR LORD'S TEACHING

    1. His own Father

    2. Father to his disciples

THE APOSTOLIC TEACHING

    1. Father of Jesus

    2. Father of believers

    3. Father of all mankind

TWO LEVELS OF FATHERHOOD

    1. Creative and biological

    2. Behavioural and moral

GOD IS THE COMPLETE PARENT

    1. He embraces qualities of motherhood

    2. He is head of the human family

Chapter 8

God's Fatherhood

As Sovereign Lord, God is also a strong' affectionate and supremely caring Father. His fatherly role expresses, indeed, his sovereign rule and must be thought of in close association with it. Sovereignty without fatherly love and care produces an image of a harsh tyrant while fatherly love on its own can mean a rather 'soft' image that neglects the realities of God's moral government of the world and of man's accountability before him.

God's relationships to creation, like his attributes, are one package. No more can we abstract sovereignty and fatherhood from each other than we can separate holiness from love or omnipotence from omniscience. Indeed, as we can refer to God's attributes under the term holy-love, we could think of his relationship with creation in terms of sovereign-fatherhood.

Scripture itself carefully maintains this balance, presenting God's providence in terms both of sovereign rule and of fatherly care. The roots of its presentation of God's fatherhood are in the Old Testament but it is only in the New and particularly in Christ that we find the full revelation. Thus Jesus taught his disciples to address God as Father and to request that his rule be as real on earth as in heaven.

> 'Our Father in heaven
> hallowed be your name,
> Your Kingdom come
> Your will be done
>   on earth as it is in heaven'

Look up Mt. 6:9-10, 11:25, 13:43, 25:34, 26:29.

OLD TESTAMENT PRESENTATION

The Old Testament has a number of statements which speak of God as Father. In one or two instances there is a close link with God's creatorhood but in every case the reference is to the relationship he sustains to his chosen people Israel. He is their Creator and Father and there is no suggestion that they thought of him as Father of the entire human race.

Sometimes, however, Malachi 2:10 and the passage it echoes, Deuteronomy 32:6, are taken as implying that God's fatherhood is as universal as his creatorhood. Certainly both passages have fatherhood and creatorhood side by side in a parallelism which virtually equates them - the Creator is Father and the Father is Creator. However, the context of both passages restricts their reference to the chosen or covenant people. Malachi was addressing his fellow-Jews when he asked his double question

> 'Have we not all one Father?
> Did not one God create us?'

The 'we' and 'us' refer not to mankind in general but to Jews who were profaning their covenantal position before God. It is even possible that in these passages the verb *'create'* refers not to the original creation of man (Genesis 1 and 2) but to the creation or establishment of a covenant people through God's call to Abraham and that the word 'Father' is used of the One at whose behest that covenant relationship had been initiated. God's people could look up to him as their Creator, the One to whom they owed their national existence, and as their Father, the One who always acted in a fatherly way towards them.

At the same time the Israelites thought of themselves as God's sons or as God's children. And God thought of them as his children and was grieved when they failed to behave appropriately.

Look up Ex. 4:22-23; Pss. 68:5, 103:13; Isa. 63:16, 64:8; Jer. 3:19, 31:9; Hos. 11:1-2.

OUR LORD'S TEACHING

The word 'Father' was a favourite with our Lord when he spoke to or about God. He used it some seventeen times in the Sermon on the Mount and more than fifty times in John 14-17. He did, however, use it at two levels.

1. His own Father

First and foremost he used it to refer to his own relationship to the first person of the Trinity - God was Father and he was Son. This emphasis has already been examined in our discussion of the Triune Nature of God [Chapter 4, §5.1] and need not be repeated here.

2. Father to the disciples

Secondly, he used it to refer to the relationship of God to his disciples - they were to think of him as 'Father' and of themselves as his sons or his children. It is with the expression of this relationship that we concern ourselves now.

Jesus clearly and constantly taught his disciples to behave according to God's will so that they might be sons of their Father in heaven - indeed, so that they might be perfect as their heavenly Father is perfect. At the same time he taught them that they should always trust God for the supply of the necessities of life. As their heavenly Father, God knew their needs and made provision for them as surely as, or more surely than he did for the birds or the flowers. Similarly, when the disciples would find themselves arrested and questioned by civil authorities because of their faith, they could rely on the

Spirit of their Father speaking to them and giving them what to say.

Some of our Lord's parables portray both erring as well as penitent and believing people as God's children. This could suggest that our Lord extended the implications of God's fatherhood beyond the godly. The prodigal son and the elder brother in Luke 16 and the disobedient son in Matthew 21 were still sons despite the offences they committed. The reference to God as Father in Jesus response to the Samaritan woman could imply that Samaritans as well as Jews were entitled to think of him as Father. Nevertheless it is generally accepted that Jesus, like the Old Testament, presented God's fatherhood purely or, at least, mainly in terms of his relationship to those in covenant with him. He did, however, change the definition of God's children from Israel as a biological and racial entity to a new people headed up in the group of twelve he had called to be his disciples.

In the great discourses of John 14-16 and the prayer that follows them in chapter 17, Jesus again and again speaks of God as Father - as 'the Father' and as 'my Father'. In the message sent through Mary to his disciples after his resurrection he spoke of ascending to his Father and to their Father - '... I have not yet returned to the Father. Go ... to my brothers and tell them, " I am returning to my Father and your Father, to my God and your God."'

The various references to God as Father bring us great insight into the nature and character of God. Indeed many of the divine attributes can be traced in the adjectives and the adjectival clauses qualifying the title or describing the activities of its holder. He is kind and good to all; he is perfect in all his ways; He is all-knowing, all-powerful; he is living and life-sustaining, loving, holy, righteous and merciful. Little wonder Christian thinkers are agreed that our Lord infused into Biblical religion a deeper revelation of the fatherhood of God than had previously been revealed or understood.

Look up   Mt. 5:45,48. 6:4,6,8,9:18, 10:19-20; 18:10-14,19,
21:28-32; Mk. 11:25-26, 14;36; Luke 6:36; 15:11-
31; John 4:23; 14-17, 20:17.

THE APOSTOLIC TEACHING

1. Father of Jesus

The Apostles clearly learned the lessons our Lord had taught about God's fatherhood. Every epistle of Paul begins with a greeting wishing grace and peace to come to the readers from God, the (or our) Father, and his Son, the Lord Jesus Christ. Every other epistle, except Third John, has the same expression or one very similar to it. 'Father' had become a normal title for the first person of the Trinity. He is the God and Father of the Lord Jesus Christ.

Look up Rom. 1:1-3;1Cor. 1;3; 2Cor. 1:2-3; Gal. 1:1 etc.

2. Father of believers

For the apostles God is uniquely their father - they often spoke of him as 'our Father'. Twice, indeed, (Rom.8:15; Gal.4:6) Paul used the Aramaic word *'Abba'* to focus on the sense of family which belongs to those who are true disciples. Stimulated by the presence and the activity of the Holy Spirit they can look up to heaven and address God in the most intimate way as 'Abba' (meaning, 'Father' or 'Daddy'). Jesus had used the same affectionate address in the Garden of Gethsemane and the assurance of Scripture is that in moments of stress we, like him, can breathe 'Father' (=*'Abba'*) to one we know most intimately and who waits to minister to our need.

Look up Rom. 6:4; 1Cor. 8:6; Gal. 1:4; Eph. 1:17; Phil. 4:20; Col-3:17; 1Thes. 3:11; Heb. 12:9; Jas. 1:27; 2Pet. 1:17; Jude 1.

3. Father of all mankind

The apostles, in contrast to both the Old Testament and, indeed, our Lord, presented God as in some sense the Father of the entire human race. The first evidence of this appears in Paul's speech at Mars Hill in Athens. He did not, in fact, use the word 'father' but he implied it by referring to his pagan Athenian hearers and to himself and his colleagues as *offspring* of the Lord of heaven and earth.

This speech is a most interesting example of how the apostles addressed hearers who had no knowledge of the Old Testament Scriptures. Indeed it is precisely at that point - the evangelisation of pagan Gentiles - that the truth of God's universal fatherhood became important. It was a vital bridge which Paul was able to use to make contact with them and to lead their thoughts in the direction of the true God, the Lord of heaven and earth.

The point of most concern to us is that God is presented as the source and sustainer of the life and breath of all men. All are dependent - completely dependent - on him, a fact which Paul found to be in accord with words of a Greek poet who said, 'we are his offspring'. The poet may have spoken more than he understood but he spoke truth - men, all men are God's offspring. They are therefore his children, his sons and in relation to them he is Father.

In the Epistle to the Ephesians the same thought seems to be in Paul's mind when he says, 'I kneel before the Father from whom the whole family (literally 'fatherhood'- Greek, *patria*) in heaven and on earth derives its name.' The point seems to be that God's relation to the human race is the original and true fatherhood, that on which earthly fatherhood is based. He is the arche-type of all fatherhood, the Father preceeding all fathers.

This is simply another way of stating that God is creator and that he sustains an ongoing relationship - a fatherly relationship - with his creatures. It does mean, however that, while the focus of Scripture's presentation of God's fatherhood is in relation to those he calls into covenant with himself (i.e., Israelites in the former age and believers in the new one), we must not think of it solely in those terms. He is in a very real, a creative, sense the father of all and in that same sense all men are his children.

Look up Acts 17:24-28; Eph-3:14-15.

TWO LEVELS OF FATHERHOOD

We have then two strands of thought, one that says God is the Father of all and one which majors on a particular fatherly relation with those he calls out from the world to be his own people, a relationship that seems to exclude those not so called.

At the same time we have our Lord's statement that at least some of his hearers could not legitimately claim to be God's children. These are particularly strong in the great debate with Pharisees recorded in John 8 and in which they claimed first to be descendants of Abraham (vv. 33 and 39) and then more ultimately to have God alone as their father - 'The only Father we have is God himself' (v.41). Our Lord's response to this was to say,

> 'If God were your Father, you would love me, for I came from God and now am here. ... You belong to your father, the devil and you want to carry out your father's desire. ...

114

He who belongs to God hears what God says. The reason
you do not hear is that you do not belong to God.'

Clearly we have something of a problem in trying to reconcile
the apostolic idea that God is father of all men with the
teaching of Jesus that some of his hearers were not sons of God
but of Satan.

The solution would seem to lie in the fact that fatherhood and
sonship are not always used in the same way. Sometimes a
biological parent-child relationship is in view and when applied
to God the emphasis is on his position as the creator and
originator of life. In this sense he is Father of all men. At
other times a spiritual or moral relationship is in view and is
like that of the wise teacher of the ancient world who was
'father' and his pupil or disciple was his 'child' or 'son'. In this
sense Joseph was father to Pharaoh and Paul was father -
spiritual father - in relation to the Corinthian believers. Equally
according to Paul, Abraham, the model man of faith, was father
to all who had similar faith even if they had no biological line
of descent from him.

Spiritually and morally the Pharisees with whom our Lord held
debate did not have God but the devil as their father. They
were doing the things their own father did - doing the things the
devil does, lying and the like - and they were not doing the
things God would have them do - in this case loving the one he
had sent. The situation is then that all men are God's sons and
he is their father in a creative sense. Their biological and
psychical life derives from him. Spiritually and morally (that
is, in terms of a spirit to spirit relationship with him and in
terms of behaviour) God is only father and man is only son
when man commits himself to God and to his ways, and does in
fact produce godlike behaviour - Thus those who make peace,
who act for the well-being of others, who love their enemies
and pray for those who persecute them, act in a godlike way

and, as a result, are recognised as 'sons' of their 'Father in heaven.'

Behind this situation lies, of course, the event recorded in Genesis 3. Sin entered human life, man fell from the estate of perfection in which he was created and as a result was driven out of the garden and deprived of communion with God. The spiritual relationship was broken and once that happened morality deteriorated, men ceased doing things according to God's pattern, they turned to their own way and in spiritual and moral terms were no longer entitled to claim to be God's sons.

However, the creative relationship remained. God was still the source of man's life and in that sense was and is Father, but man had forfeited the important spiritual and moral aspects of his sonship. Like the prodigal in our Lord's parable, man, the sinner, has no claim on God's fatherly care - He has sinned and deserves only God's wrath. His only hope is that God would be gracious and grant him forgiveness and restoration of the spiritual fellowship lost through the Fall. This, is what God did in choosing Abraham and those in covenant through him and this is what he has done in bringing men and women to salvation and to sonship in Christ.

The father's grace to the prodigal son in our Lord's parable is a perfect illustration of the position. The father retained his fatherhood even after the son had deliberately forfeited all right to a position in the home. The son knew he was not entitled to return as a son - he had already claimed and squandered his inheritance - so he pleaded to be taken on as a hired servant. But, when he did come in penitence, he found that the father's grace wonderfully outstripped his sin and granted him forgiveness and a restored sonship. The father could not cease to be the parent of the prodigal but fellowship had been broken and the son was no longer following his father's behaviour patterns and so in the moral sense had ceased to be his son and had become the son of a different father.

116

The parable gives a picture of the condition of the human race. As Creator, God is Father of all mankind and can never cease to be so. Sin has, however, severed spiritual fellowship and has caused men to take their cue from Satan, the tempter, so that doing his works they can be said to be of their father, the devil. Until there is repentance and a work of grace to restore the broken relationship with God and produce patterns of behaviour that conform to his will, God is not man's father in a spiritual or moral sense. Nonetheless because he is God's creature and in a creative sense God's child he is still accountable to him. The great blessing of the Gospel, as we shall see, is that men can be delivered from the realm of Satan and into the Kingdom of God and into a new sonship and a new way of life.

Look up   Gen. 3:1-19, 45:8; Mt. 5:9, 44-45; Lk. 15:11-24; Jn. 8:31-47; Rom. 1:18-35, 4:16-17, 5:12-19; 1Cor. 4:15; Gal. 3:29.

It would be quite natural at this point to begin to examine the gracious acts undertaken by God to restore sinful men to fellowship with himself and to the holy living such fellowship entails. Some theologians do in fact discuss those acts of divine grace as expressions of the fatherhood of God, but it is probably better to take them separately reminding ourselves that, as Father, God planned and effected our salvation. No more can we separate his saviourhood from his fatherhood than we can separate his fatherhood from his sovereignty. That we treat these matters as distinct topics is simply to facilitate the limited capacities of our own minds.

We have considered God's role as Father and at several points have referred to Scriptures which draw a parallel between God our heavenly Father and human fathers. Some of these passages have also made reference to human mothers and raise questions about whether or not God should be thought of in a mothering as well as in a fathering capacity.

GOD IS THE COMPLETE PARENT

1. He embraces qualities of motherhood

There is very little femininity evident in the references to God in Scripture - masculine forms are consistently used. Nonetheless a clear analogy with motherhood does occur in response to an accusation by his people that God had forsaken and forgotten them. Even though a mother might forget her child, the Lord, their 'creator', will not forget them. He will be a true mother to them. That God could use the mother model to emphasise his own fidelity seems to suggest that he regards the analogy as appropriate and that he can be thought of as Israel's mother as well as its Father.

What needs to be remembered is that in Hebrew, as in English and other languages, masculine words often served for the common gender and so were used to embrace both male and female. The word 'Adam', meaning man, is an example. Similarly, father can stand for ancestor or forefather and can include within itself all that we mean by motherhood. It is then more or less equivalent to our word parent. Thus when the Bible speaks of God as Father it may - or sometimes may - include within its thought the idea of motherhood.

Even more telling is the fact that at creation God made man - male and female - in his own image. The human man and woman, father and mother, are types of which God is the archetype. It seems necessary then to think of God as embracing in himself all that is implied by both genders and therefore all that is implied in fatherhood and motherhood. He is father in the sense of being the complete and ultimate parent. What is divided into two roles in human life is one in him.

To deny the mother role to God, as some Christians do, (sometimes in reaction to feminist views that would make God female) seems a monumental insult to the human female. The implication seems to be that she is some sort of inferior accessory to the male. In fact, God created her as a full and vital part of his image. His image is not in the male alone or in the female alone but in both together. The woman's motherly functions must then reflect on earth an element of the divine life that is as essential as the male role of fatherhood. In a sense, God is the complete parent, father and mother in one.

Look up Gen. 1:26-27; Isa. 49:14-15.

2. He is head of the human family

Our picture of fatherhood is, of course, that of a father in a human family. We must be careful, however, lest by transfering this to the divine being we effectively make him out to be nothing more than some kind of superman. We would then have fallen into the trap mentioned in the Psalm, 'You thought I was altogether like you' (Ps. 50:21b). The truth is that human fatherhood is modelled on the divine amd not the reverse. God is the archetype, the real father and human fathers are at best but pale reflections of him.

Nonetheless there is a real analogy between the two in Scripture and we are therefore justified in drawing parallels and in seeing in the best of human fatherhood some indication of the glory of his fatherhood. At the same time we have another highly significant picture in what has been revealed to us of the relations within the trinity. What God the Father was and is to Jesus tells us much about what he is and can be to us.

One of the most obvious things about fatherhood in Biblical times is headship. He, who was a father in the normal human sense of the term, was head of his family. At the same time a person, who was a teacher of others, was similarly in a position of headship over his disciples or pupils. Such headship carried with it considerable authority.

In the ancient world a father's authority was a jealously guarded privilege. His wife (or wives) and his children had to acknowledge him as head of the family and had to obey him as their master.

An ancient Israelite law provided that parents could even bring a rebellious son before the elders who could order capital punishment by stoning. This prevented the father from taking such drastic action on his own initiative, but its main intention was to support parental authority and purge out the evil of rebellion against it. It shows how important fatherly authority was, not just for the men of the day, but for the divine author of the law. The same is true of the teaching of the Book of Proverbs.

> Listen to your father, who gave you life'
> and do not despise your mother when she is old

The Lord Jesus in his own life on earth showed real respect for the authority of Joseph, the husband of Mary, who was legally, if not biologically, his father. We read that after the visit to Jerusalem when he had remained with the teachers in the temple, 'he went down to Nazareth with them (Joseph and Mary) and was obedient to them' (Luke 2:51). But it was in his relationship to the first person of the trinity, the Father, that his respect for paternal authority is most evident. Though he was God the Son, he was yet subordinate to his Father. He spoke of himself as sent into the world by the Father, as taught by the Father, as doing the will of his Father, as doing nothing apart from the Father. In short, he recognised that the Father's position in relation to himself as the Son was one of authority.

In his teaching, Jesus emphasised the ultimate authority of God the Father. A key petition in his pattern prayer is, 'Your will be done on earth as it is in heaven'. Indeed, for him the vitally important thing in life is to do the will of the Father. Those who do so are in a family relationship with himself - 'Whoever does the will of my Father in heaven is my brother and sister and mother'. Only such as do so will find a welcome into the eternal kingdom of heaven.

Preaching in Athens Paul proclaimed God as creator of everything and as the Lord of heaven and earth. The Father, who is Lord in this sense, is clearly in a position of authority and is the One to whom men owe their obedience. James defines the religion that God our Father accepts as pure in terms of submissive obedience to God's authority and will - 'to look after orphans and widows in their distress and to keep oneself from being polluted by the world'.

As King and as Father, God has supreme authority. There is none greater than he, none beyond him to whom he can or must appeal or give obedience. Ultimate authority is his privilege and is inherent in his being God, the Father, the Lord of heaven and earth.

Look up Deut. 21:18-21; Prov. 23:22-23; Mt. 6:10, 7:21, 12:50, 26:39,42; Lk. 2:51, 22:29; Jn. 6:57, 8:16, 8:28, 7:17, 15:15, 20:21; Acts 17:24-28; Gal.,1:4; Heb.,10:7,9; Jas. 1:27.

9 God as Father

CARING FOR HIS CHILDREN

1. Loving them
2. Providing for them
3. Protecting them
4. Training them
5. Communing with them

HONOURED BY HIS CHILDREN

1. With appropriate respect
2. With acceptable worship
   1) Devotion
   2) Adoration
   3) Obedience
   4) Penitence
   5) Trust
   6) Intercession
   7) Service

Chapter 9

God as Father

CARING FOR HIS CHILDREN

1. Loving them

God's choice of and his ongoing care for Israel were motivated by love. His sending of the Lord Jesus was motivated by love - 'God so loved the world that he gave his one and only Son.' His love was extended to us even when we were in sinful rebellion against him, when we showed no love towards him.

The Greek New Testament has a unique word for love. It is *agape* and refers neither to physical attraction nor sensual experience but to a caring concern for the well-being of others, a concern which is always turned into caring action. This word and its associated verb - *agapaõ* - are rarely found outside the New Testament where they are used both of God and of the lifestyle to which Christians are called. 'God', says John, 'is love' (*agape*). Love is his essential nature. He is concerned for and acting for the well-being of his creatures. He loves them when they are in rebellion against him or in submission to him. He loves them when they are in difficulty and when they are enjoying ease and prosperity. 'He is love.' 'He so loved the world that he gave his one and only son that whoever believes in him shall not perish but have eternal life.'

Love is the very essence of his fatherhood and his supreme motivation as he discharges his fatherly responsibilities.

Look up Deut. 4:37, 7:8-9, 10:15, 23:5; Neh. 9:17; Ps. 103; Jer. 31:3; Hos. 11:1; Jn. 3:16-17; 1Thes. 2:16; 1Jn. 4:7-11; Rev. 1:5.

The great pattern of love - fatherly love indeed - is, of course, in the relationship obtaining between the first and the second persons of the Godhead. The Father's love for his only Son was expressed clearly both at the baptism of Jesus and at his transfiguration - 'This is my Son, whom I love, with whom I am well pleased.' This love is such that he could commit all things to the hand of the Son. Our Lord spoke of his own love for his disciples as of the same order - 'As the Father has loved me, so have I loved you'. His great desire voiced in the prayer of John 17 was that his disciples should enjoy God's fatherly love to the full.

Look up Mt. 4:17, 17:5; Jn. 3:34-35, 10:17, 15:9, 17:23-26.

2. Providing for them

At an earlier stage we noted Biblical evidence for the provision God makes for his creatures. That material (Chapters 5, §4, and 6) need not be repeated here but what does need to be said is that it is as Father that God so provides. The air we breathe, the food we eat and the water we drink are provisions he makes as expressions of his fatherly love. Jesus could tell his disciples not to worry about such things because God, their heavenly Father, knew that they needed them and could be relied on to supply them. He reminded them that, though they had natures that were essentially evil, they knew how to give good gifts to their children and said that this was a pointer to God's bounteous fatherly provision - 'How *much more* will your Father in heaven give good gifts to those who ask him.'

Look up Mt. 6:25-34, 7:9-12; Jn. 10:14-18; (cf Ps. 23 where the shepherd is provider).

3. Protecting them

Every father has an inexorable duty to protect his children, particularly in the years before they reach maturity and independence. God accepts that responsibility in relation to his children, none of whom ever reaches full maturity in this life. Late in life even Paul, the great apostle, was still pressing on towards it (Phil. 3:12).

We see God protecting Noah and his family from destruction by the flood. We see him protecting Lot from the destruction of Sodom and Gomorrah. We see him protect the patriarchs from famine. We see him protect Israel in Egypt, in the wilderness, and in the land of Caanan. We read of his righteousness intervening to deliver and thus to protect the oppressed from those who oppressed them.

The great factor assuring God's people of his protection was his presence with them. Thus Jerusalem was regarded as safe while God dwelt there. But, when he withdrew his presence, enemies could conquer it and destroy even its sacred shrine, the Temple. Thus Ezekiel in vision saw the glory of the Lord depart from the temple and was able to warn his fellow-exiles that Jerusalem was no longer protected. The great hope of the prophets was of restoration and the renewal of God's presence with and protection of his people, first in the return from exile and then in a more ultimate sense in the incarnation of the Son (Immanuel, God with us) and in the sending of the Spirit.

Look up Lev. 25:18-19; Deut. 12:10, 33:28-29; 1Kgs. 4:25; Isa. 40:9-11; Jer. 23:6; Ezek. 34:27, 48:35; Zech. 14:11.

The Psalmists and the prophets often sang of the Lord's protection. They spoke of him as their rock, their refuge, their fortress, their shield, their keeper, the one in whom they had safety. Their words have been very precious to believers down the centuries and have given them assurance of the Lord's power to protect them from every danger.

The apostles of the New Testament period had assurance of the Lord's power to keep them in every situation of life. Paul, on board ship and in a terrifying storm, had the assurance of God's protection not just for himself but for all on board - 'I urge you to keep up your courage, for not one of you will be lost ...' When the same apostle stood, apparently alone, to defend himself before Caesar, he knew that the Lord stood with him. When finally he did feel that death was approaching, he was still assured of the Lord's protection - 'I ... am convinced that he is able to guard what I have committed to him for that day.'

Look up 2 Sam. 22:1-4, 47; Pss .4:8, 18:1-3, 31:1-5, 46:1-3, 62:5-8, 89:26, 91, 115:9-11, 119:114, 121, 144:1-2; Jn. 6:36-40, 10:27-29, 17:12; Acts 27:22-23; Rom. 8:38-39; 1Thes. 5:23-24; 2Tim. 1:12; Jude 24

4. Training them

In Ancient Israel there was a strong emphasis on fathers training their children - especially their sons - in the tenets of faith and wisdom. Earliest training was largely in the hands of mothers but fathers were required to pass on to their sons the stories of God's past dealings with Israel together with explanations of their religious observances and duties. They also gave their children as much general education as they could and in particular trained sons in their own trades or crafts. Jesus, brought up in the household of Joseph, was trained as a carpenter. Paul was trained as a leather worker. A child had to be prepared for life and it was the duty of its parents and at many points of its father to do so. The New Testament continues the emphasis - 'Fathers, ... bring them up in the training and instruction of the Lord'.

Look up Ex. 10:2, 12:26, 13:8; Deut. 4:9, 6:7,20-21, 32:46; Prov. 1:8, 4:1-9, 6:20; 22:6; Eph. 6:4.

Again the pattern of a human father training his offspring is but a reflection of that real fatherhood, from which all fatherhood is derived (Eph. 3:14-15). To speak of God as Father is an acknowledgment that those who do so are under God's training, that he is preparing them for life, not merely here on earth but in the life to come.

The vicissitudes of life, its ups and downs, its joys and sorrows, its prosperities and its adversities all contribute to the making of a man of God. Job, for example, had great prosperity and then fell into adversity. He suffered terrible loss and deep doubt and near despair but then he came face to face with God. Indeed, it was only through the distress of adversity that he was made ready for the brokenness of heart and will before the Lord that were essential to blessing. He was being trained in the deep experiences of life. The same was true of Paul and the illness or weakness he regarded as a thorn in his flesh.

The Lord is often presented as a teacher who instructs his pupils in perfect wisdom. He guides the humble in what is right, teaching them his ways. When God became incarnate in the Lord Jesus, he came as a teacher. Jesus taught his disciples on the mountainside. He taught in the synagogues and in the temple. He taught with authority, that is, on his own authority and not like the Scribes who always appealed to and quoted their great scholars. Listening to his wisdom, his logic, his parables, men were compelled to acknowledge that he was unique - 'No one ever spoke the way this man does' was the verdict of temple-guards sent to arrest him but unable to do so because they themselves were arrested by his words. Jesus declared his role on earth to be a matter of doing the works of his Father. So in his teaching he was simply giving expression to God's fatherly role of instructing and training men.

The exposition of the place of discipline or chastisement in Hebrews 12 shows how God uses it to train his children.

> Our fathers disciplined us for a little while as they thought best; but God disciplines us for our good, that we may share in his holiness. No discipline seems pleasant at the time, but painful. Later on, however, it produces a harvest

of righteousness and peace for those who have been trained by it.

Look up   Ex. 4:12,15; Pss. 25:4-12, 27:11, 80:11, 119:12,64, 108,135 etc.; Isa. 2:3, 48:17; Mt. 4:23, 5:1-2, 7:29, 13:54, 26:55; Jn. 7:46; 2Cor. 12:7-10; Heb. 12:3-17.

5. Communing with them

We hear a great deal these days about failure in communication between parents and their children.

In our first study we noted that God can be known and that knowing him is not merely a matter of knowing facts about him but of a one-to-one, person-to-person, spirit-to-spirit communion. The point is that he draws near to us - indeed that he comes to dwell within us - when we become believers and as a result communion between him and the human soul or spirit is established.   John could well write, 'Our fellowship (or communion) is with the Father and with his Son, Jesus Christ'. We enjoy that fellowship but it is God who makes it possible. Our Father in heaven is not a far away unapproachable God but one who draws near, who enters communion with us allowing us to know him and giving us in that knowledge the life that is eternal.

God's fatherly care is such that he maintains his presence in the soul with a view to real and continuous communion. Because he has sent his Spirit into our hearts such communion is always immediately open to the believer. If it does not take place, the fault is ours in that we allow the things of earth and more particularly the desires and the worries of self to fill our minds and deflect our interests from him.

Jesus promised that the Spirit would guide the disciple into all truth and make the things of Christ known to him. The Spirit is the divine communicator.   He effects and maintains communion between the divine and the human. He assures the believer that he has been adopted into God's family and can address God as Father. He helps our weakness in prayer by interceding for us in terms that we may not understand but that accord with God's will. He it is who makes God's fatherhood real in our experience.

Look up Jn. 16:13-15; Rom. 8:9-17,26-27; Gal. 4:1-7; 1Jn. 1:3.

HONOURED BY HIS CHILDREN

1. With appropriate respect

It is a fundamental axiom of life that children honour - and should honour - their parents. If parents are responsible to love and care for their children and, if they honestly do so, they are surely entitled to be respected and honoured by their children. In the divine revelation the position of fathers and mothers is safeguarded by the fifth commandment - 'Honour your father and your mother ...' This command is re-iterated several times in the New Testament and clearly relates to something of the utmost importance. It goes with the Father's love as the 'reverse' side of the relationship that binds him to them.

As Father, God expects to be honoured. His position as creator and originator of life and as the Father, who has called men into a living relationship with himself means that he deserves honour. He deserves to be glorified. Eli was chastised for neglecting to honour him and the men of Malachi's day had to face searching questions, because they were despising God's name, walking in ways that defamed rather than glorified the one who was indeed their Father.

How different the attitude of the Psalmists whose great concern was to honour or glorify the Lord. They called on descendants of Jacob to honour and revere him, to ascribe to the Lord glory and strength, to sing to the glory of his name, to speak of the glorious splendour of his majesty. Isaiah has a similar challenge calling on men to give glory to the Lord and indicating that it is for his own glory that God has created them.

One way in which we honour our parents is by spending time with them - reciprocating the time and the communion they granted us in earlier years. And in the relationship between believers and God it is essential that time is spent in his presence. This means talking to him in private prayer - going into one's own closet to commune with one's Creator and Redeemer. It means taking time to listen to what he says through his word - time to read, ponder and take on board the truths and the standards he has revealed for our benefit. And it also means taking time to engage in these exercises in the company of other believers - participating in corporate prayer and in listening to the reading and the preaching of his word.

Our Lord himself was deeply concerned that God should be honoured first by himself and then by others. 'Father'. he prayed, 'glorify your name', and again, 'glorify your Son, that your Son may glorify you'. He said that he would respond from heaven to his disciples prayers so that he, the Son, might bring glory to the Father in doing so.

In criticism of the outward formalism of the Pharisees and to urge a proper attitude of worship that would bring honour to the Father, He quoted Isaiah's words about people honouring God with their lips and not their hearts

The Apostles were equally concerned that their own ministries and the lives of those to whom they wrote should glorify or honour their heavenly Father. On a host of occasions they express the prayerful wish that glory might come to God the Father. The great ' Hallelujah' cry of Revelation 19:6-7 does not use the word Father, but it is clarion clear in its call to give glory to the Lord.

Hallelujah!
For our Lord God Almighty reigns.
Let us rejoice and be glad
    and give Him the glory.

Look up   Ex. 20;12; 1Sam. 2:27-33; Pss. 22:23, 29:1-2, 66:2,
145:5; Isa. 42:8,12, 43:7, 45:10-12; Mal. 1;6; Mk. 7:6
(cf., Isa. 29:13); Jn. 12:28, 14:13, 17:1; Rom. 11:33-
36; Gal. 1:5; Eph. 1:14, 3:21; Phil. 1:11, 2:11, 4:20;
1Tim. 1:17, 6:16; Jude 24-25; Rev. 1:5-6.

2. With acceptable worship

Paul urged his readers in Rome to offer themselves in the
entirety of their persons as living sacrifices to God.

'Therefore, I urge you, brothers, in view of God's mercy, to
offer your bodies as living sacrifices, holy and pleasing to
God - which is your spiritual worship (AV - your
reasonable service)'.

What, we may well ask, does worship really involve? What
should a Christian be and do to make the kind of response that
will be pleasing to God, that will give proper recognition to his
supreme worth?

To answer these questions adequately would entail a wide-
ranging study far beyond our present brief. Suffice it to say
that Christian worship involves -

1) Devotion

The Scriptures constantly declare God's love for his children.
In return those children are expected to be devoted to him in
sincere love. The crucial command imposed on Israel and
endorsed by Jesus as the first and greatest of all the
commandments is, 'Love the Lord your God with all your heart
and with all your soul and with all your strength. The great
tragedy of ancient Israel was that their love for the Lord was

132

often weak or non-existent. The Lord could say, 'When Israel was a child, I loved him and out of Egypt I called my son ... I led them with cords of human kindness, with ties of love.' But at the same time he had to say, 'But the more I called Israel, the further they went from me. They sacrificed to the Baals and they burned incense to images.' In a word God's love for them was not requited as it should have been. Instead their love was given to false gods that were no gods at all.

After the resurrection, when Jesus met his disciples beside the Sea of Galilee, the crucial question for Simon Peter was, 'Do you truly love me ...' Jesus wanted Peter to acknowledge that he really loved him and would be totally devoted to him. Peter, who so recently had betrayed the Lord answered, 'Yes, Lord, you know that I love you.'

Writing to the Corinthians Paul pronounces an anathema on those who do not love the Lord. Clearly he assumes and expects that his readers were people who loved the Lord. In his final greeting to the Ephesians he says, 'Grace to all who love our Lord Jesus Christ with an undying love.' He expected an unwavering devotion to the Lord, a love that did not ebb and flow, a love that would not die. The writer to the Hebrews tells his readers that help they rendered to fellow Christians was an expression of love to God. Peter could tell his readers that though they had not seen the Lord Jesus they loved him. John warns against professing to love God and denying that profession by failing to love a brother man - 'if anyone says, "I love God," yet hates his brother, he is a liar.' The apostle continues the theme and insists that those who love God show that love by obeying his commands - 'This is love for God; to obey his commands.'

The apostolic message endorses then the teachings of the Old Testament and of Jesus that God expects his people to love him and to give to him the prime devotion of their hearts.

Look up   Deut. 6:5; Hos. 11:1-4; Jn. 21:15-17; 1Cor. 16:22;
          Eph. 6:24; Heb. 6:10; 1Jn. 4:19-5:3.

2) *Adoration*

Adoration is reverential homage given to one regarded as
worthy of love and devotion, one, who is appreciated for his
worth.   Because the other person is greatly valued the heart
reaches out to him in gratitude and in ascriptions of praise and
glory.   Adoration thus embraces devotion, thanksgiving and
praise. Its aim is to give honour and glory to God.

As far as human language can take us we articulate in words
what we think of God.   We tell him we are amazed as we
contemplate his greatness.   We tell him we love him.   We thank
him for his grace and praise him for all he is and for all he
does. Like the Psalmist we sing,

> Praise the Lord, O my soul
>   all my inmost being, praise his holy name'
> Praise the Lord, O my soul,
>   and forget not all his benefits—
> who forgives all your sins
>   and heals all your diseases,
> who redeems your life from the pit
>   and crowns you with love and compassion ...

Like the heavenly choir in the Book of Revelation we sing,

> You are worthy, our Lord and God
>   to receive glory and honour and power,

Look up   Ex. 15:1-18; Deut. 32:3-4; 2Chr. 6:14, 7:3; Pss. 8; 36:
          5-9; 77; 103 etc. Lk. 2:46-55,67-79; Rom. 16:25-27;
          Eph. 3:20-21; Jude 24-25; Rev. 4:11; 7:12; 15:3-4.

3) *Obedience*

Worship entails receiving, considering and heeding the word of
God.   The important thing is that, coming from the God we

adore, the word is applied carefully to our own lives. We are not to be 'hearers only' but 'doers also'. As John puts it so clearly, those who say they love God are expected to keep his commandments - if they say they love him and do not obey him they are liars.

Obedience to God's word involves submission to God himself. Such submission is resisted by our fallen natures and many a tussle goes on between a Christian's own will and what he knows to be God's will. Like Paul, he has to say, 'what I do is not the good I want to do; no, the evil I do not want to do—this I keep doing.' It is only as we submit to God's will, as we yield control of our lives to God, that we truly give him the worship - the worthship - that is due to him.

Look up Ps. 119:9-16, 105-112; Mt. 7:24-27; Lk. 8:18; Rom. 6:15-23, 7:7-25; 2Tim. 3:14-17; 1Jn. 4:19-5;3

4) *Penitence*

Those who worship God and who get close to him become acutely aware of their own shortcomings and sin. Like dwarfs in the presence of giants they see how far they are removed from the holiness of God and like Isaiah cry out, 'Woe to me, I am ruined; For I am a man of unclean lips ... ' It is thus, in confession of sin, in turning from sin that men come to faith in Christ and it is thus that we must always walk before him. Penitence is not just for the beginning of the Christian life; it is the Christian life-style - 'just as you received Christ Jesus as Lord' (i.e., in repentance and faith) 'continue to live in him.'

Confession of sin and a genuine turning away from it is thus part and parcel of the devoted Christian's relationship to the Lord. He knows that there is an inclination towards evil in his heart and that, even though he knows the Lord and knows his sins forgiven, he has unworthy thoughts and performs unworthy acts. As he contemplates the God he adores, whose worth he appreciates, he becomes penitent and turns away from those

135

sins confessing them to God and seeking and finding his forgiveness. He looks to God to purify his heart, to preserve him from future sins and to establish him in ways that are righteous.

Look up Neh. 9:1-3; Job 42:1-6; Pss. 32:1-5, 51:1-17, Lk. 13:3-5; Acts 2:38-39, 17:30, 19:18, 26:20; Col. 2:6; Jas. 5:16; 1Jn. 1:9.

5) *Trust*

Any positive person-to-person relationship requires that each person trust the other. Trust is placing reliance in something or in someone. Those who truly know God trust him. They accept his promises as true. They know him to be faithful and know that in all the ups and downs of life he works for the good of those who love him.

Trust is, of course, an expression of faith and it is interesting that in the New Testament belief is often spoken of as moving out from the believer towards, to, into or upon the one in whom he trusts. Faith is not the mere acceptance of facts. It is commitment to a person. Thus we believe into the Lord Jesus Christ and through him place our trust in God. 'Through him', says Peter, 'you believed in God, who raised him from the dead and glorified him, and so your faith and hope are in God'. A Christian is one who, day by day and to the end of his days, reposes his trust in God. That trust is a vital element in worship, in a Christian's response to the God he knows.

Look up Gen. 15:16; Ex. 14:31; Pss. 39:7, 71:5; Jn. 3:16,18,36, 9:35; Acts 10:43, 19:14; Rom. 9:33, 10:11; Gal. 2:16; 1Tim. 1:16; 1Pet. 1:8,21; 1Jn. 5:13.

6) *Intercession*

When there is real trust between two persons one can ask the other for help and can expect to receive the help he needs. Those whose trust is in God have the inestimable privilege of being able to approach him to present their petitions, to ask him to supply what they need and can do so in the confidence that he will do just that, that he 'will meet all their needs according to his glorious riches in Christ Jesus'.

The Bible abounds in assurances that God hears and is ready to answer the prayers of his people. His ears are attentive to the cries of the righteous. Jesus told his disciples that if two of them agreed about a petition it would be done for them by his Father in heaven. He promised those who would remain in union with himself and in submission to his words that, if they asked what they wished, it would be given to them.

Prayer that brings that kind of response from God must, of course, be in harmony with God's will. No-one can expect God to act out of harmony with his own will but, lest harmony with that will should seem beyond us, one of the ministries of the Holy Spirit in the believer is to stimulate and articulate just such prayer - 'the Spirit helps us in our weakness ... the Spirit intercedes for the saints in accordance with God's will.'

Prayer is not, however, to be limited to one's own needs. Jesus prayed for his disciples and for those who would believe through their work. The apostles prayed for one another and for those to whom they ministered. Paul urged Timothy that as a matter of priority 'requests, prayers, intercession and thanksgiving should be made for everyone.' Then he added, 'This is good and pleases God our Saviour, who wants all men to be saved and to come to a knowledge of the truth.' James tells us that the prayer of a righteous man is powerful and effective.

The believer prays to the God he knows as a matter of privilege and as an expression of his worship, his acknowledgment of God's supreme worth.

Look up   Ps. 34:15; Mt. 18:13; Jn. 15:7; Rom. 8:26-27; Phil. 4:19; 1Tim. 2:1-4; Jas. 5:16.

7) *Service*

A relationship of personal trust means that one can request service from those who are in the relationship. Man's response to God's demands is what we call 'service'.

As Sovereign Lord, God is entitled to every service his creatures can render. As Redeemer he has absolute rights over the lives of those he has redeemed. They are his bondslaves even if in another sense they have freedom of a unique kind, Their supreme duty is to serve him, to prosecute his causes among their fellows and to be always ready to respond to his directions. His servants do and always should serve him.

The Israelites of old were to serve him alone and were to do it with all their hearts. Men are to serve him with awe and trust and with gladness. Jesus set a marvellous example - he came to serve and was among men as one who served, in the very nature of a servant. Paul also thought of himself as a servant of God and of his converts in Thessalonica as those who had turned from idols to serve the living and true God.

Service rendered to God is true worship, an acknowledgment of the Lord's sublime worth and supreme authority. Because of who he is and of his relationship to him, the Christian, cannot but serve him. Paul's counsel to the believers in Rome becomes the guiding principle of his life - 'never be lacking in zeal, but keep your spiritual fervour, serving the Lord.'

Look up Deut. 6:13, 10:12; Pss. 2:11, 100:2; Mk. 10:15; Lk. 22:27; Rom. 1:9, 12:1-2,11; Phil. 2:7; 1Thes. 1:9; 2Tim. 1:3.

10 God's purpose to save

1. HIS DESIRE TO SAVE

2. HIS COVENANT TO SAVE

    1. An eternal commitment

    2. Electing grace

3. HIS COMPETENCE TO SAVE

    1. His unlimited power

    2. His righteous character

    3. His incomparable grace

Chapter 10

God's purpose to save

HIS DESIRE TO SAVE

The enigmatic threat addressed 'to the serpent' in Genesis 3 is generally regarded as the first good news in the Bible. It asserts that God would one day cause the offspring of woman (i.e., a human person) to defeat the serpent and reverse the damage done at the Fall.

> I will put enmity between you and the woman
> > and between your offspring and hers
> he will crush your head,
> > and you will strike his heel

This promise is developed and expanded as the divine revelation unfolds. It finds fulfilment in Christ - when the time had fully come, God sent his Son, born of a woman, born under the law, to redeem those under law, that we might receive the full rights of sons.'

Throughout Scripture God presents himself as desiring salvation for men, as One who takes no pleasure in the death of the wicked but is pleased when they turn from their evil ways and live. He called Abraham and in doing so chose Israel to be the recipients of his redeeming love. His desire was to save. In the New Testament Paul tells us that God wants all men to be saved and Peter assures us that he is patient, 'not wanting anyone to perish but everyone to come to repentance'.

Clearly then the wish, the desire, the purpose of God is that men be saved. He is not a capricious despot seeking either the annihiliation or the eternal torment of those who offend him. He is rather a gracious loving father who desires that no one perish and who has taken steps to turn his desires into real salvation achievements - He has saved and he does save.

Look up   Gen. 3:15; Deut. 7:6-9; Ps. 106:1; Isa, 43:3,11,15,21, 60:16, 63:8; Ezek. 18:23; Hos. 13:4; Lk. 16:10; 1Tim. 1:1, 2:3-4; Tit. 1:3, 3:4-5; 2Pet. 1:1, 3:9; Jude 2,

'Why', we may ask, 'does the Lord desire to save men? Why is salvation needed?' The answer is that all through Scripture man is presented as perverted by sin and incapable of ever attaining to the standard of righteousness required by God. Sin entered the stream of human life through Adam and brought the penalty of death on the entire race.

The biblical teaching on man's nature and sinfulness requires detailed separate treatment. Here we can only assume the broad conclusions of such treatment and affirm that as a result of the Fall man is separated from God, is under penalty and liable to eternal death. He is unable by his own effort to gain a real relationship with God. He is without God, without hope and desperately needs divine intervention to bring him salvation.

The salvation man needs is not merely a deliverance from the everyday or the exceptional difficulties of life. It is salvation from the thraldom and the consequences of the sin that pervades his entire nature and that leaves him guilty before God.

Look up   Gen. 8:21; Isa. 59:2; Jer. 2:22, 17:9; Jn. 3:36; Rom. 3:10,23, 5:12-19, 6:23; Eph. 2:12.

It in against this background that God reveals himself as Saviour. He is God the Saviour. When he sent his Son to be incarnate in human flesh, it was to save men, to save his people from their sins, to save those who were lost. Quickly Jesus became known as 'the Saviour' and it was as such that the apostles delighted to proclaim him. Risen from the dead and taken up to heaven, he is

141

at God's right hand as 'a Prince and a Saviour'. He is 'Christ Jesus, our Saviour' - the one in whom and by whom alone there in salvation.

Look up Ps. 106:21; Isa. 43:3, 45:5, 49:26; Mt. 1:21; Lk. 19:10; Jn. 3:16; Acts 5:21; 1Tim. 1:1-4; Tit. 1:3, 2:10; 2Pet. 1:1; Jude 25.

HIS COVENANT TO SAVE

The Bible presents God not only as desiring to save men but as actually committing himself to do so. He has bound himself by solemn promise and the usual way of referring to this commitment is in terms of 'his covenant'. He has covenanted to save men and in the outworking of his purposes brings those he saves into a unique 'covenant' relationship with himself. His covenant to save men entails:-

1. An eternal commitment

Before the universe came into existence or man was even created, God committed himself to save men. If he is eternal and omniscient, as indeed he is, he knew the end from the beginning and it is impossible to believe other than that his commitment to save is as eternal as he is himself. This being so the writer to the Hebrews can use the phrase, 'the eternal covenant', to refer to the Lord's unchanging commitment to save men.

God's commitment found expression in human history as he again and again promised or covenanted salvation to men. Particularly important are the promises he made to Abraham and his descendants, promises which find their fulfilment in Christ and in those who through faith become 'Abraham's seed' and inheritors of the promised salvation. By making solemn promises God, who is totally truthful and can never deny himself or fail to keep his word, bound himself in covenant to provide salvation and its benefits for men.

In harmony with the idea of an eternal covenant are those New Testament Scriptures which assert that the Christian is not just a person who suddenly without any antecedent cause puts his faith in Christ. He is, in fact, a Christian by virtue of the fact that God had chosen him and thus had committed himself to him before the world was even created. The salvation God effected in Christ was the outworking of his eternal purpose and would not have been provided apart from that eternal - and gracious - commitment.

We can see further evidence of this covenantal commitment in a number of statements made by the Lord Jesus in relation to his own ministry. In the main these are found in John's gospel and affirm that he was doing the will - fulfilling the commitment - of the one who had sent him. We can, indeed, speak of a covenant within the Trinity under which the Father and the Son committod themselves to the saving work in which Jesus was to engage.

Look up Eph. 1:4, 3:7-13; Heb. 13:20; 2Pet. 3:9.

Many theologians speak of God's deliberate purpose to save men - his commitment to salvation - in terms of what they call 'the divine decree'. The word *decree* occurs in the English versions of Psalm 2 verse 7 - 'I will proclaim the decree of the Lord' - and is usually understood as meaning that God planned certain activities and sovereignly marked out their course according to his own will and without being subject to pressures or influences arising from outside of himself,

That he *decreed* the bounds of the sea and the orbits of the planets can be accepted without difficulty by those who believe in his creatorhood. When, however, *decree* is used with reference to the salvation of men's souls, controversy quickly comes to the surface. Believers, to whom the freedom of the human will is precious, find it hard to accept the idea that God's saving purpose is effected through an eternal and, apparently, an unalterable decree.

One element in the problem is the rather autocratic or dictatorial undertone inherent in the English word 'decree'. The Hebrew word - *'choq.'* - in rather softer and means 'a *marking out'* or a *'prescription'*. Any writer wishing to imply that a particular divine prescription had a permanent or an inflexible character had to add an adjective or a short clause to make that permanence clear.

Thus in Psalm 148:6 we have a decree (a *'choq'*) 'that will never pass away' and in Jeremiah 5:22 we read of an everlasting barrier (a *'choq'*) that the sea cannot pass. Since the word *'decree'* is not so qualified in Psalm 2:7, we must be careful that, when we use the English word *'decree'* for God's commitment to salvation, we do not invest his will and his person with an autocratic inflexibility that is alien to other elements in his self-revelation.

As we know him through the Scriptures, he deals with men as a loving father deals with his children and he does so on the basis of one moral personality (his) interacting with other moral personalities (theirs). He always gives full respect to men's personalities and never treats then as mere robots. He is far far more than a puppeteer or a super-technician sitting at some all-embracing control panel!

While we must accept the assertions of Scripture about the sovereign and effective will of God, we must at the same time accept other Scriptures which affirm or assume a considerable degree of human freedom and which declare God's right to change his mind and, in response to the stances of men, adapt his prescriptions and his programmes as he deems necessary.

We must also avoid the temptation to build our theology by the remorseless application of human logic to one group of passages while neglecting or over-riding the other group. This being so and in order to safeguard the fact that our God is loving and kind rather than cold clinical and despotic, it is preferable to think of his commitment to save men in terms of *'covenant love'* rather than in terms of a 'decree'. The great fact on which we must focus and for which we must give to the Lord our heartfelt thanks and our adoring worship is that he really committed himself to our salvation. That commitment in as eternal as he is and has been wonderfully put into effect in the person and work of Christ and through the presence and work of the Holy Spirit.

Look up Jer. 18:1-10; Heb. 3-1:6.

2. Electing grace

As we study Scripture and indeed as we reflect on human life, it is clear that the experience of salvation is not universal. All men do not have the light of revelation, the joy of redemption, the life of the regenerate or the hope of ultimate restoration. All men do not know the Lord.

Scripture tells us clearly that God bestows the benefit of his salvation selectively to some and not to others. The Biblical words which refer to his selection are 'election' and 'choosing'. Abraham was chosen for God's special purposes of grace. Jacob was chosen in preference to Esau and his descendants became God's chosen people. When the Israelite nation became apostate an elect or chosen remnant was preserved faithful and continued to exist right through to New Testament times.

Jesus himself spoke of those who belong to God's kingdom as 'chosen' ones. He asserted that all those given to him by his Father would come to him, words that imply prior planning and prior decision that some would come to him. The apostles spoke and wrote freely of Christians as God's elect or chosen ones. Paul went so far as to assert that the choice was made not in time but before the world was created. Those so chosen by God are said to be predestined to be united to Christ and to share the salvation inheritance provided in and through him.

Many people do not like the doctrine of election but, if we would be true to Scripture we must receive it humbly as part of God's revelation. We must, of course, hold it in balance with other revealed truths but we will nonetheless hold it. At this point in our studies we affirm it as an expression of God's sovereign kingly rule.

Those, who are privileged to enjoy God's saving grace, can do no other than join the apostle in giving adoring praise to him who has chosen - elected - them to salvation.

> Praise be to the God and Father of our Lord Jesus Christ ...
> For he chose us in him before the creation of the world ...
> In love he predestined us to be adopted as his sons through
> Jesus Christ, in accordance with his pleasure and will— to
> the praise of his glorious grace, which he has freely given
> us in the One he loves.

Look up   Ps. 105:6; Isa. 45:4; Mt. 22:14, 24:20-21; Jn. 6:37,
15:16; Rom. 8:29,33; 9:10-13,20,21, 11:5; Eph. 1:4,
11-14, 2:8; Col. 3:12; 2Tim..5:21; Tit. 1:1; 1Pet. 1:2,
2:9; Rev. 17:14.

The biblical dosctine of election raises a number of difficult theological questions - questions that have baffled great minds across the centuries and that still baffle us today. Without professing to be able to answer ultimate questions we will look briefly at some of the issues in the next chapter.

HIS COMPETENCE TO SAVE

It is wonderful to know that God desires to save men and that he committed himself to do so even before the world was created. But from our point of view it is important to be assured that he is actually able to fulfil his intended goal.

To help provide that assurance and at the risk of some overlap with earlier studies, we focus on:-

1. His unlimited power

Discussing the 'omnipotence' of God we noted a number of passages asserting that absolutely nothing is beyond possibility so far as he is concerned - 'with him all things are possible'.

When we examine the saving acts of God we discover that they are always expressions of his sovereign power. Salvation is God exercising his sovereign power for saving purposes.

The deliverance of the Israelites from Pharaoh's Egypt provides one of the most obvious examples. Moses commanded the people to stand firm and see the deliverance (the salvation) the Lord would bring. And they did see a demonstration of God's great power as they crossed the Red Sea on dry land and looked back to see their enemy's army overwhelmed by the returning flood of water. Later writers, prophets and psalmists looked back to that deliverance and used it as a picture, a type, of new deeds of salvation God would yet effect. Isaiah had it in mind when he predicted the deliverance of those Jews who were taken into captivity in Babylon. He vividly described what God would do for the exiles by using words taken directly from the exodus story. The return from exile would be a new exodus, a new manifestation of God's sovereign power.

The salvation effected by Christ is similarly presented as a manifestation or a series of manifestations of God's power. The very birth of Jesus without the involvement of a human father was a work of a God to whom all things are possible. His sinless life and his incomparable teaching alike displayed that power. But supremely it was displayed in the resurrection. No mere man could return from death. No wonder-worker could produce resurrection. But God raised Jesus from the dead. This was the miracle of all miracles and the vindication of Jesus as Son of

God and the Saviour of men. So great was its impact that Paul often referred to God as the one 'who raised Jesus our Lord from the dead'. The thing that matters for our purposes just now is the incomparably great power that God exerted in Christ when he raised him from the dead.

To talk of God's Saviourhood, of his saving works, is to assert his sovereign power and his complete competence to work out and fulfil his saving intention. Thought of in this way saviourhood is an aspect of God's kingly rule and has, of course, been given some consideration in the context of our discussion of that topic (Chapter 7).

Look up Ex. 14:13; Pss. 66:5-7, 74:12-17, 78:9-55, 81:l0, 98:1-2, etc.; Isa. 11:16, 41:17-20, 42:14-16, 48:20-21, 49:8-12, 51:10-11, 52:1-12; Jer. L6:l4-15, 23:7-8; Mic. 6:4-5, 7:15; Mt. 19:26; Mk. 10:27; Lk. 1:37; Rom. 1:4, 4:24, 8:11; 1Cor. 6:14; Gal. l:l; Eph. 1:18-20.

2. His righteous character

In the Old Testament there is a very close link between God's saving acts and his righteous character. His saving acts are acts of righteousness. Indeed sometimes words like 'righteous' and 'righteousness' seem to be virtually synonymous with 'salvation'. The Lord is at one and the same time 'a righteous God and a Saviour', one who calls on men to turn to him for salvation and who makes his promises in all integrity or in real righteousness so that it can be said of him - 'In the Lord alone are righteousness and strength'. The point in that just as he has the power, the sovereign power to save, so he has the moral excellence, the righteousness of character essential to that role.

In the New Testament the righteousness of God in clearly asserted. Indeed Paul insists that the gospel itself is an expression of that righteousness. The death of Christ, a sacrifice of atonement on behalf of sinful men, took place to demonstrate

God's justice or righteousness. And Christ himself, the incarnate Son of God, maintained that perfect righteousness while here on earth - he had no sin of his own and he suffered and died as one who was absolutely righteous - 'the righteous for the unrighteous'.

The idea that God is light, so prominent in the writings of John, is in many ways just another way of saying that he in righteous. There in no darkness of sin, of injustice or unrighteousness in him and the One he sent as Saviour could truly say, 'I am the light of the world'

The one who is perfectly righteous, who always does right, is truly competent to bring men the salvation they need - deliverance from the darkness of unrighteousness and into the light of truth and righteousness.

Look up   Gen. 18:25; Isa. 45:21-25; Jn. 1:1-9, 9:5, 12:35-36,46, 17:25; Rom. 1:17, 3 25; 2Cor. 5:21; Heb. 4:15; 1Pet. 3:18; 1Jn. 1:5-7.

One aspect of God's righteous character - his faithfulness or fidelity - is particularly important at this point. Before the creation of the world God made himself liable to covenant obligations and committed himself to man's salvation. Such a commitment would be of no value at all if it were not fulfilled. Man would then be left in his sins and subject to the penalty due for them. But this is not the case. God is faithful. His word stands for ever. It is eternal and unbreakable and faithfully kept. It is his guarantee. All his promises are honoured. He fulfils his undertakings and as a result the salvation to which he covenanted himself has become a reality. He is faithful and he is just or righteous,

Look up   Num. .23:18-19; Deut. 7:9; Pss. .36:5, 92:1-2, 119:90; Isa. 25:1, 40:8; 1Cor. 1:9; 2Cor. 1:20; 1Thes. 5:24; Tit. 1:2; Heb. 6:18; 1Jn. 1:9.

3. His incomparable grace

In our discussion of the divine attributes we defined grace as 'that love of God which bestows benefits and ultimately salvation on men and women who deserve no such favour.' At this point we simply affirm that it is this love, this supreme and incomparable grace, that makes our God truly competent to save men. As sinners accountable to a Holy God we need his grace if we are to be saved from our sin and its guilt. Thus reminding ourselves of that fact we can go on in chapter 12 to focus on the experience of God's grace, which believers are privileged to enjoy.

11 God and election to salvation

THE PARADOX OF ELECTION

  1. Foreknowledge and foreordination

THE PURPOSE OF ELECTION

THE PROBLEM OF REPROBATION

  1. 'What they were destined for' 1Pet. 2:8b

  2. 'Objects of his wrath—prepared for destruction Rom. 9:22

  3. 'men whose condemnation was written about long ago' Jude 4

SUMMING UP

Chapter 11

God and election to salvation

THE PARADOX OF ELECTION

We have seen that Scripture clearly teaches that God sovereignly wills that some men be saved and that his will to save those men is not frustrated. Whoever he predestines, he calls and justifies and sanctifies and in the end glorifies. His sovereign will secures all that he purposes and salvation is therefore to be credited entirely and unconditionally to his electing grace.

Alongside the Scriptures which affirm God's unconditional election of some men to salvation we find others which stress man's responsibility to and accountability before God. The commands of God impose moral and spiritual obligations - 'You shall love the Lord your God ...', 'You shall love your neighbour ...', 'Repent', 'Believe in the Lord Jesus', and the like. Such commands imply that man has freedom to obey or disobey and that his enjoyment of God's favour is somehow conditional on his response to them. If man is free to make moral choices, and if in any way God takes account of those choices in the application of his saving grace it would seem that those choices and the person's behaviour decide whether or not he experiences God's salvation. If he heeds God's word he will be saved. If he ignores or rejects it he will be lost.

Clearly Scripture presents man as accountable for his actions and as carrying blame or guilt if he fails to respond to God's commands and to God's grace. Even those who have no special revelation of the law or the gospel are without excuse if they fail to grasp what can be known of God through the physical universe. Scripture strongly emphasises that God will reward men according to their works - those who do good and seek glory, honour and immortality will receive eternal life and those who are self-seeking, who reject the truth and follow evil will receive wrath and anger. It is those who actually call on the Lord, who confess with the mouth, 'Jesus is Lord,' who will be saved.

Down the centuries Christians have grappled with the problem raised by the two distinct strands of teaching found in Scripture. Some have swung to one extreme or the other, being so taken up with God's sovereignty that they fall over backwards into fatalism or so taken up with man's freedom and his ability to choose that they virtually eliminate God's sovereign rule all together. Others have tried to synthesise the two ideas and produce middle of the road theologies but in doing so they too have neglected, denied or perverted some vital emphasis.

What has baffled great minds will not be solved in the context of this study. What we can say is that both strands of teaching are in Scripture and are to be humbly received in faith. Both must therefore be held in paradox, that is, as apparently contradictory teachings which our minds cannot reconcile or unify but which are nevertheless received and affirmed as true. As so often our highest wisdom is to acknowledge that God's thoughts are higher than ours and that there is deep mystery in a sovereign rule that expresses itself in electing grace and that nonetheless allows men freedom to accept or reject his approaches and his saving provisions for them.

Look up Mt. 25:31-46; Jn. 3:14-18, 5:24; Acts 2:24; Rom. 1:20, 2:6-11, 9:30-10:4, 10:9.

1. Foreknowledge and foreordination

Paul and Peter both associate God's electing grace with his foreknowledge (see God's Attributes. Chapter 2. Section 6. Omniscience). This is often taken to mean that God knew in advance who would be righteous or who would heed the gospel and on that basis predestined such to be saved. Such an interpretation seems to make salvation depend on some goodness in the recipient and is hard to harmonise with Scriptures which teach that men have no merit before God and that he saves solely on the basis of his own love and grace. In any event to say that God chooses on the basis of his foreknowing how generations yet unborn would behave, does not solve the problem of election. It merely pushes it a step further back and in a way deepens the mystery!

On our canons of logic (inevitably inadequate when handling ultimate mysteries), if God foreknew anything about us even before human life began, what he foreknew must have been fixed before that event, otherwise it could not have been fore-known. Since no one else existed then, he must have been the One who fixed it. If then he knew that some men would respond in a particular way, he must have pre-ordained that they do so - and that is, in fact, exactly what is meant by predestination or election to salvation. The problem remains - it is not solved!

The truth seems to be that, being omniscient, God has a prior and an eternal knowledge of everything and using criteria which he alone knows, he has been disposed in love to appoint some men to salvation. Because the criteria of selection is in God and not in men themselves, no one who enjoys God's salvation can ever have valid grounds on which to boast. He can only acknowledge that he has been saved by the grace, the unmerited favour of God.

THE PURPOSE OF ELECTION

We usually think of election as a divine choice that destines the soul for heaven rather than hell. That is, of course, true but, as we read Scripture, we find that very often a prior goal - a Christ-like life here on earth - gets prominence.

Jesus told his disciples that he had chosen them that they might go and bear fruit that would last and in the context the fruit they were to bear was love of the kind he had shown them - 'Love each other as I have loved you.' Paul wrote of God predestining those he foreknew 'to be conformed to the likeness of his Son that he (the Son) might be the first born among many brothers.' The purpose of election is, then, that there might be a host of men and women whose lives are modelled on that of Jesus. Peter has the same idea when he addresses his readers as 'chosen ... for obedience to Jesus Christ and sprinkling by his blood'.

A similar principle had operated under the old covenant with ancient Israel. God chose the nation not because its people were better or more numerous than others but simply because he loved them. But his purpose in choosing them was that they might live in a way that honoured him, by keeping his commands and loving him with their whole hearts. Election was not just a matter of great privilege, it was with a view to a God-honouring quality of life, something that Israel, alas, too often failed to produce.

Election and predestination are not then theories to be debated but the basis of a life to be lived. God's purpose is that anyone he chooses for himself should live as did the Lord Jesus Christ, honouring the Father, loving his neighbours and giving his all in self-effacing service. The proper Christian response is to bow before the Lord in thankful praise and in total self-sacrifice.

Look up   Deut. 6:1-20, 7:7-11, 10:12-22; Jn. 15:9-17; Rom. 8:29; Eph. 1:3-14; 1Pet. 1:2, 2:9.

3. The problem of reprobation

The major objection that arises against the doctrine of election focuses on the implication that by choosing some sinners for salvation God was automatically not choosing others or, alternatively, he was choosing those others not for salvation but for perdition.

On our canons of logic it is hard to avoid the conclusion that if God, knowing all that can be known about every single human being, chooses some to be saved, he thereby decrees - either directly or indirectly - that the remainder suffer doom.   To many sincere Christians that conclusion seems to be out of harmony with the picture of a God of love who loves and is longsuffering with his creatures.

By being treated differently those who are saved and who, as much as others, deserve God's wrath avoid it and do so, it seems, on a basis of a divine choice that is independent of their spiritual and moral condition.   They do not deserve salvation but they get it and others, no more guilty than themselves, do not get it.   To many people it seems quite unjust that God's attitude to the elect is in such stark contrast to his attitude to others.   He seems to love the one and not to love the other.

One response to this dilemma is to argue that all men are sinners and deserve his ultimate wrath and therefore that those who are not saved are not treated unjustly - they get their due desert.   'God's wrath comes on those who are disobedient.' (Eph. 5:6, cf. Jn. 3;36; Rom. 1;18; Col. 3:6 etc.).   The response of some who emphasise God's sovereignty and the unconditional nature of his promises is to interpret (or re-interpret) 'God loved the world' as meaning 'God loved the elect', and then to say that he had no saving love for those not elected to salvation. Some theologians do not hesitate to limit God's love in that way. Logic drives them to do so, but we need to ask if, in fact, Scripture teaches what they believe.

Three passages need to be considered:-

1. *'Objects of his wrath—prepared for destruction,*
Romans 9:22-23

The words - 'objects of his wrath — prepared for destruction' at the end of verse 22 - have often been taken as implying predestination to perdition (the Greek, apōleia, means loss, wasting, destruction, ruin etc.).

The first thing to notice is that the sovereignty of the divine will and of divine authority dominates the context - the potter can do as he pleases with the clay and the clay has no right to question what he does. Ths second thing is that the words in question are part of a hypothetical question, 'What, if God ... ?' Paul may, therefore, be imagining a situation and defending God's right to act in a certain way without actually saying that the situation would ever exist or that, if it did, God would act in that way. In the context, God is certainly presented as making choices between those on whom his purposes of election rest and those on whom he bestows no mercy and who are therefore outside the promised inheritance.

Words like 'hating' (v.13) and 'hardening' (v.18) are used of those who are not chosen to be recipients of mercy but they need not necessarily carry the implication of deliberate divine election to perdition. The verb 'to hate' (miseō) often highlights indifference or relative disregard towards one party in contrast to great interest in, or love for, another party. Thus God loved Jacob and hated Esau but, while Esau did not experience Israel's blessings, he was not destroyed and his descendants lived on to prove the fact. Malachi, at the end of the Old Testament era knew them (the Edomites) well and one of their families, the Herods, proved more than a thorn in the flesh to the Jews in our Lord's day.

In the third place, Romans 9 is concerned with the unbelief of Israel, an unbelief that gave Paul great pain of heart. The whole thrust of his argument is that God's promises relate not to all the descendants of Abraham or Isaac but only to a small remnant who, together with Gentiles of like faith, are 'called' to be God's people. What Paul seems to be saying in v.22 is that a vast mass of Israelites are outside of God's electing purpose and so are not God's children and not the children of promise who can be regarded as Abraham's (true) offspring (cf. v.8). Paul's proof texts, Isaiah 8:14 and 28:16, are exactly those used in 1Peter 2:6 and 8, and in their original use clearly point to Jewish rejectors of true righteousness.

In the fourth place, Paul does not say that God prepared those of whom he spoke for destruction. Many think that this is implied but, when we read to the end of the chapter, we discover that the focus of the argument turns on the identity of those who pursue righteousness. Those who obtain it do so by faith and those who do not obtain it are those who pursue it by law, i.e., the Jews with their religion that put law-observance above faith. They were in error simply because they did not pursue righteousness by faith (v.32). In failing to do so they stumbled and clearly bear responsibility or, at least, some considerable responsibility for their own fate:

In the light of these considerations it seems extremely precarious to assert that those who eventually meet perdition do so because God has predestined them to that fate.

2. 'They disobey the message whichis also what they were destined for' 1Peter 2:8b

Peter had been speaking of men who stumble because of disobedience and then added the words, 'which is also what they were destined for' or more literally 'to which they were appointed'. Some people understand this as teaching that God appointed or pre-destined the disobedient to eternal perdition

Peter's words do seem to say that stumbling and presumably also any consequences resulting from it happen by divine intention. In verse 6 the same verb is translated as 'lay' (I lay a stone in Zion) and clearly means a deliberate act of divine appointment. The assertion in verse 8 will then be that God has pre-appointed, has ordained, has decreed that some men will stumble in disobedience and unbelief in contrast to others who believe and to whom Christ becomes precious.

In part, the difficulty with Peter's statement arises from the fact that his main aim is to encourage believers to mature in the kindness of the Lord. He does not explain what he says about the unbeliever and, because this is the case, any interpretation we make will be somewhat speculative. He might, for example, mean that part of the God-ordained experience of those as yet unconverted is to stumble, perhaps even to stumble frequently over the truth. But in saying that he need not necessarily mean that such would never be able to repent or enjoy salvation. He might, on the other hand, have been thinking that God's plan was that Jews as a national entity be cut off from grace in order that the gospel might spread to Gentiles. Indeed, the very next verses, 1Pet. 2:9-10, would support such a view by talking about Christian believers as God's new nation. In that event, as Romans 9, 10 and 11 make clear, there is the possibility of repentance and of those, who had been out off, being re-grafted into the tree of God's purposes.

It should also be noticed that Peter does not in fact say that those appointed to stumble are appointed to perdition. He is not, it seems, even thinking of destiny in the passage but is rather concerned with the problems of maintaining Christian joy and Christian standards in a world that opposed and persecuted believers. It would, therefore, seem to be improper exegesis to regard Peter's words as teaching predestination to reprobation.

3. *Men whose condemnation was written about long ago ...* *Jude 4*

Jude mentions men, 'whose condemnation was written about long ago'. The Greek verb (prographō) means 'to write in advance' or 'in public' (cf. Rom. 15:4; Eph. 3:3). It does not have the force of pre-ordain as is implied by the Authorised (or King James) Version which reads, 'who were before of old ordained to this condemnation'. The reference is rather to a condemnation foretold in writing but not or, at least, not necessarily, to a condemnation (literally a 'judgment') involving eternal perdition.

Jude is thought by many to be alluding to 2Peter 2 and simply saying that the condemnation of the ungodly persons, whose advent caused him to write was already predicted in writing in that passage. Others think he is saying that the ancient prophets had written in advance of the condemnation that was prescribed for the ungodly. Either way we would have to conclude that Jude is certainly not saying that God has predestined anyone to perdition. Indeed, we must also point out that he does not in any way spell out what the condemnation of which he is thinking will entail.

NOTE It is sometimes thought that Proverbs 16:4 teaches election to perdition, or as it is sometimes called, 'double predestination' - 'the Lord works out everything for his own ends - even the wicked for a day of disaster'. In fact, the Hebrew word translated 'disaster' is *ra'a* which often means nothing more than ;adversity' or 'trouble' (e.g. Job 2:10; Ps. 23:4; Isa. 45:7). In the context (v.6) it is clear that the disaster in the sage's mind is not final and could

160

be avoided by a change of heart. Predestination to reprobation is not in view.

SUMMING UP

To sum up, it seems reasonable to affirm that we must stand on the solid facts of what God has said and not on deductions or inferences we might make beyond them. The facts are that predestination/election based on God's free and sovereign choice is taught in Scripture and so is the doom of the ungodly for whom, equally in God's sovereignty, perdition is reserved. But the idea that God has specifically destined anyone to that fate is not required by any text in the Bible.

We certainly encounter real difficulty when we apply our minds to these problems. Our highest wisdom is to accept the plain assertions of Scripture as they come to us and to avoid attempting reconciliations that are beyond us. We must leave the relation between the fate of the reprobate and God's sovereign rule as something shrouded in the mystery of things beyond our ken.

12 God's Incomparable Grace

THE REALITY OF HIS GRACE

    1. In Old testament History

    2. In the person and work of Christ

    3. In the experience of believing men

HOW TO BECOME ONE WHO KNOWS
THE LORD

    1. Repentance is essential

        1. A change of attitude

        2 A change of direction

    2 Christ is the only way to God

DO YOU KNOW THE LORD?

Chapter 12

God's incomparable grace

THE REALITY OF HIS GRACE

Throughout Scripture God is presented as incomparable in grace. His love for his creatures is such that he meets and more than meets their need for salvation. And he does so not as a response to merits in men, but as the bestowal of free unmerited favour. He does so in grace. He gives generously. He gives without counting the cost. He gives to the uttermost and holds back nothing as he moves savingly into the sphere of human life.

We have already discussed his power to save - nothing is impossible to him if he wills to do it. What we are saying here is that *he has the will to save* and that he turns that will into saving action.

The reality of his saving grace is seen throughout Scripture and in the experience of believers through the centuries. Put in the briefest of terms we see it in three phases—

1. In Old Testament history

In the Old Testament God's grace showed itself in the choice of men to positions of privilege in fellowship with himself and in acts of kindness undertaken to help his people in times of need.

He chose and called Abraham and in him chose the nation of Israel to be his privileged people. He did this, not because of merit in those chosen, but on the ground of his own love - his grace. When his people became oppressed he helped and saved them. When they came under alien control and their lives were subject to forfeiture he redeemed them.

The exodus from Egypt is a prime example of his redemptive salvation. Israel was in bondage and God in grace brought then through the Red Sea and into freedom. Subsequently during the period of the judges and the kings he again and again delivered them from oppression.

In the later books of the Old Testament the twin hopes of redemption from captivity in Babylon and of deliverance from the enslaving grip of sin become prominent and again the motivating factor is God's grace - he bends over backwards, as we might say, to reach men and show mercy to them. In grace he also promised a new covenant with his law written on and his Spirit resident in men's hearts, inclining them to keep his statutes. He was working, always working to save men and in doing so was moved by love alone, by sheer and incomparable grace. The exercise of that grace is the reality that dominates Old Testament history.

Look up Deut. 7:6-8, 33:3a; 2Chr. 9:8; Pss. 5:12, 30:5, 89:17, 106:4; Isa. 60:10.

2 In the person and work of Christ

God's plans to save men were, as we have seen, a matter of divine commitment or covenant. Those plans entailed the Son, the second person of the trinity, coming to earth to participate in human life, to disclose more of God's nature and love, to die on the cross in order to pay the debt due by men on account of sin, to rise again on the third day as the conqueror of death, man's last enemy, to ascend to the Father's right hand as the glorified God-man, as both Lord and Christ.. Then he sent the Holy Spirit in a new way at Pentecost and subsequently into the hearts of all who believe in him.

165

That these plans were carried out is evidence of God's supreme grace. Men did not and do not deserve such care and such sacrificial action. They deserve only wrath but God, again in sheer grace, loved those who were at enmity with him to the extent of giving his only begotten Son to save them. The Son himself gave up the glories of heaven for a time and accepted the limitations of a human body in order to be able to offer the ultimate sacrifice to save men.

But for grace, the grace of God, the grace of our Lord Jesus Christ, there would have been no salvation such an we know today. It is God's incomparable grace that enables men to enjoy his salvation.

Look up Lk. 2:4; Jn. 1:17; Acts 15:11; Rom. 3:24, 4:16, 5:15-17; 2Cor. 12:9, 13:14; Eph. 2:5-8; Phil. 2:6-8; 2Thes. 2:16; Tit. 2:11, 3:7; Heb. 4:16; Jas. 4:6.

3. In the experience of believing men

God's grace is continually demonstrated as he brings men to salvation through faith in Christ. Those who, in apostolic times, turned from idols or from Jewish traditions to serve the living and true God were, in fact, saved. They knew themselves to be redeemed and forgiven and reconciled to God. They were justified and sanctified and had a sure hope that one day they would be raised and glorified to share an eternal inheritance in heaven. And the same has been true of multitudes in the centuries since then.

But there is another dimension to the experience of those whom God saves. He sends his Holy Spirit into their hearts and thus makes himself present in their lives. This presence of God in the believer's life brings untold benefit - real communion with God, control of behaviour, bestowal of gifts, instruction in the truths of God and of Scripture, to name but a few.

Look up Jn. 14:26, 15:26, 16:5-15, Rom. 8:26f; Gal. 5:22-24.

Grace is a reality now as it was in Bible times. It is a reality in the experience of every saved sinner, of every true believer.

> 'Twas grace that wrote my name
>> In life's eternal book;
> 'Twas grace that gave me to the Lamb,
>> Who all my sorrows took.

> Grace taught my wandering feet
>> To tread the heavenly road;
> And new supplies each hour I meet,
>> While pressing on to God.

But in so extolling grace let us always remember that it is God, the One who is gracious, whose love abounds and transcends every need, who is to be praised. Grace is an attribute of his being, not an independent entity in its own right. We must be careful to ensure that our worship is directed not to grace as an abstract quality but to God, the One who is ever gracious, the One who bestows surpassing grace and who is always able to make all grace abound to us' (2 Cor. 9:8).

If God's incomparable grace is not yet part of your experience it can become so. The next section is written with the sincere wish and prayer that any reader who does not yet know the God of all grace will be encouraged and helped to seek and find him - that he or she might indeed become one who knows the God who has been the focus of our studies.

HOW TO BECOME ONE WHO KNOWS GOD

Jesus said in his great high-priestly prayer, 'this is eternal life, that they *may know you*, the only true God, and Jesus Christ whom you have sent' (John 17:3).

167

We get to know another person by meeting that person, by spending time in his company and by communicating each with the other on a person-to-person basis. We may or may not have known facts about him when we first met but from the first meeting onwards the knowing process involves the two factors mentioned in chapter 1 - knowledge of facts relating to the person and knowledge of the person. We can know the facts without knowing the person but we cannot know the person without at the same time knowing some facts about him. Interestingly we can meet someone about whom we know no facts at all but as soon as we meet person-to-person knowing in both senses can begin.

An important factor in coming to know another person in the ability of that person and of oneself to open up and allow themselves to be known. There has to be self-disclosure on the part of both parties. So it is with knowing God. There has to be a willingness on his part and on the part of the human soul to reveal the real self to the other and to enter into a true person-to-person relationship. So far as God is concerned he has already disclosed himself in a host of ways, but supremely in Christ. The facts are recorded in Scripture and are there to be learned by men. But more than that, God is sovereignly able to approach and disclose himself to the human soul as and when he pleases. He is not obliged to follow any set pattern and as a result men and women find themselves meeting him in a thousand different situations. His ways are often mysterious and difficult to understand but of his willingness to enter into meaningful communion with men, to allow men to know him, there can be no doubt.

What concerns us now is the human side of this relationship. Some folk have the inestimable privilege of a Christian upbringing. They learn facts about God in childhood but that does not automatically mean that they get to know him. Some do and some do not! Others have no such background yet they too meet with him, often quite unexpectedly, and without any real idea of who or what he is. In either case a knowing relationship can begin and can grow at the factual or intellectual and at the personal or emotional levels.

What, then, does Scripture say to someone who does not know God but who would like to do so, or who, at least, is sufficiently interested to investigate the possibility of knowing him? To answer that question adequately would take more space than is available in this context but we can nevertheless try to outline the essentials.

1. Repentance is essential

To repent is to turn around, to have new interests, new goals, a new mind. It involves a turning away from old interests and the repudiation of things that are evil, but the main emphasis is on turning to the new, to righteousness, to love and to God. Paul could tell the Thessalonian Christians that they had turned *to* God from idols to serve the living and true God and to wait for his Son from heaven. The turning from idols was an important part of their conversion experience but the really great thing was that they had turned *to* God, that they were serving him and waiting for the coming again of his Son. In short, they had repented.

Repentance is often understood in terms of sorrow for sin and of acts performed to put right or offset its offence. These things are part of repentance but the biblical view of repentance is broader and includes all that is involved in turning *to* God. It involves,

1) A change of attitude

Human beings have a tendency to think highly of themselves. They may boast of their parentage and upbringing, of their race or religion, and of their talents and achievements. They can be very self-reliant particularly in matters of the moral or spiritual life - they feel they know how to live and they want to do so in their own way, to be themselves and to do their own thing.

Biblical repentance involves a change in attitude. Self has to be seen as inadequate and impure and its motives and actions as earning not God's favour but his displeasure. The repentant person knows his condition and sees himself in need of some gracious provision from God. Like a pauper in the presence of a benefactor he takes the role of a dependent person. He becomes what the Lord Jesus called 'poor in spirit' (Matt. 5:3). His pride is broken, his boasting is ended. He comes to God as a needy soul with nothing in his hands and with an open heart. He looks up to God as the one who can supply all his needs, who can forgive and cleanse away his sins, who can renew and strengthen his will, who can give him new life and an eternal inheritance.

Our Lord's story of two men going up to the temple to pray wonderfully illustrates the right and the wrong attitudes. The Pharisee had an attitude of self-reliance - 'God I thank you that I am not like all other men ... I fast twice a week and give a tenth of all I get'. The Publican by contrast placed no reliance on himself. He came to God's house as a pauper and pleaded for God's mercy - 'He ... beat his breast and said, "God have mercy on me, a sinner"' (Luke 18:9-14).

2) A change of direction

Repentance involves a 180 degree turn around. It means turning towards God and beginning to live in a way that pleases him. It means continuing to live in that way.

Scripture teaches that man has a tendency to move in the opposite direction. Early man became futile in his thinking and exchanged the glory of the immortal God for images made to look like mortal man and birds and animals and reptiles (Rom. 1:20-23). He was moving further and further away from God. The prodigal son in our Lord's parable illustrates the way in which men turn their back on God. As the prodigal turned away from his father so we have all turned away from God (Luke 15:11-24). As Isaiah put it, 'We all like sheep have gone astray, each of us has turned to his own way' (Isa. 53:6).

The repentant person does a U-turn. He turns from pursuing his own way and turns towards God. The prodigal's story illustrates what is needed. He realised the hopelessness of his situation. He was empty handed and at the end of himself but he began to think of his father and of the good things of the family home. Things he had once abhorred now became attractive - if only he could get back to his father he would get fair treatment as a hired labourer! As his attitude to his father changed to one of trust, his will was strengthened and he decided to go home, to return, to make the U-turn. And he did just that - he went back. He put his new attitude into action and moved in a new direction towards a father he knew could help him. He came as a beggar. He came in poverty of spirit and he found grace and love and sonship.

So those who would know God must turn to him, must exercise their wills and seek him, must come with an attitude of believing trust and readiness to walk no more in their own ways but in his. The Thessalonians turned to God from idols. Each one of us must turn *from* the idols, whatever they are, that have a dominating role in our lives, and turn in simple childlike trust *to* him.

Repentance is not an option, it is essential to the knowledge of God and to eternal life. Again and again it was commanded of men of old. Hosea gives us a well known example, 'Return O Israel to the Lord your God' (Hos. 14:1). Our Lord called on men to repent because God's Kingdom had come to hand (Matt 4:17 etc.). He told people that unless they repented they would perish (Luke 13;1-5). Similarly the apostles preached repentance as God's primary command - 'he commands all people everywhere to repent' (Acts 17;30). Parallel with this,

171

or perhaps we should say synonymous with it. is the oft-repeated call to seek or call on the Lord. Men are told to seek him while he can be found (Isa. 55:6). They were assured that when they sought him with a whole heart they would find him (Jer. 29:13). 'Seek,' said Jesus, 'and you will find' (Matt. 7:7-8). Peter preaching at Pentecost could quote Joel to give the same assurance, 'everyone who calls on the name of the Lord will be saved' (Acts 2:21). The important thing, the vitally important thing, is to seek the Lord, to call on him and to do it wholeheartedly with a clear determination to commit oneself in faith to him and to walk in his ways, in a new direction.

2. Christ is the only way to God

At this point we must bring the Lord Jesus to the forefront of our thinking. He came to our world and into our humanity as the God-man, one who possessed both a divine and a human nature and who, through his human life, disclosed God as none other ever did or could do - 'No one has ever seen God, but God the only (Son) who is at the Father's side has made him known' (John 1:18). This being the case the more we learn about Jesus the more we know about God - 'Anyone', he said, 'who has seen me has seen the Father'.

But not only does the Lord Jesus disclose God to men, he, and he alone, introduces them to God. He could say, 'No-one comes to the Father except through me' (John 14:6). Reflecting on our Lord's ministry, Peter says, 'Christ died for sins once for all, the righteous for the unrighteous to bring you to God' (1 Pet. 3:18). The thrust of his argument is that by his death our Lord achieved all that needed to be done in order to remove the barrier separating men from God and so, now alive again and enthroned with the Father, he is able to lead men to him as a court servant might lead in and introduce visitors to an earthly king.

A number of Scriptures make the same point by speaking of men having access to God and to his grace through Christ - 'Through him (Christ), we both (Jews and Gentiles) have access to the Father ...' 'In him and through faith in him we may approach God with freedom and confidence' (Eph. 2:18, 3:12) - 'through whom (our Lord Jesus Christ) we have gained access by faith into this grace in which we now stand' (Rom. 5:2). Those to whom these statements were addressed were those who had come to God through the Lord Jesus. They had called upon him with faith, believing in him and in his power to help and save. Their faith may have been, indeed, will have been, weak and faltering but putting their trust in him they found themselves introduced to fellowship with God and brought into a relationship with him in which they knew him and know themselves known by him.

Underlying the experience of the early Christians and of the multitudes who have followed them down the centuries are the solid facts that God can be known, that he has made himself known in the Lord Jesus Christ and that by coming to Christ in faith one is brought into communion with God, into a person-to-person knowing relationship with him,

Those who are not yet in that relationship, who do not know the Lord, are missing out on the most valuable thing in life, that spiritual relationship with God for which, whether they know it or not, their souls long. Not only so but they are without God and without hope not just for this life but for the life to come. For such the next life can only be a thing of terror vividly described by Jesus in terms of a fire that does not quench, an eternal fire prepared for the devil and his angels (Mark 9:48, Matt. 25:41).

The good news is that men can escape that fate and enjoy eternal life by knowing the only true God and Jesus Christ whom he has sent (John 17:3). But, as had been said earlier, it is not a knowledge that is automatic or natural to men. We have to put ourselves in a situation in which we meet God personally and this we do by definitely and deliberately calling on him or seeking him through Christ. This we - this <u>YOU</u> - are commanded to do.

'*Come* to me. said Jesus. 'all you who are weary and burdened and I will give you rest. Take my yoke upon you and learn of me. for I am gentle and humble in heart and you will find rest for your souls' (Matt. 11:28-29).

'*Repent* then and turn to God. so that your sins may be wiped out ...' (Acts 3:19).

'*Believe* on the Lord Jesus. and you will be saved' (Acts 16:31).

'The Spirit and the bride say, "*come*" ... whoever is thirsty, let him *come*. and whoever wishes. let him *take* the free gift of the water of life.' (Rev. 22:17).

To those who obey this command. who come to the Lord Jesus and put their trust in him. there are great and precious assurances that God does a saving work in their lives. Here are some of them exactly as they are written in Scripture.

'Jesus declared, "I am the bread of life. He who comes to me will never go hungry and he who believes in me will never be thirsty (spiritual needs - appetite and thirst - will be satisfied)... whoever comes to me I will never drive away ... My Father's will is that everyone who looks to the Son shall have eternal life and I will raise him up at the last day"' (John 6:35-40).

'I tell you the truth. whoever hears my word and believes him who sent me has eternal life and will not be condemned; he has crossed over from death to life.' (John 5:24).

'Jesus said ... "I am the resurrection and the life. He who believes in me will live, even though he dies; and whoever lives and believes in me will never die ..."' (John 11:25-26).

'The word is near you: it is in your mouth and in your heart, that is the word of faith we are proclaiming 'that if you confess with your mouth, "Jesus is Lord", and believe in your heart that God raised him from the dead you will be saved. For it is with your heart that you believe and are justified, and it is with your mouth that you confess and are saved ... for everyone who calls on the name of the Lord will be saved.' (Rom. 10:8-13).

This, then, is the Gospel, the good news that men can be saved, can be sure of eternal life and can know God and be in a relationship of communion with him through faith in the Lord Jesus Christ.

Do you know the Lord?

If you don't or, if you are not sure, then look again at the Scriptures quoted above. Let the word of God be your teacher - humble yourself before him, abandon your reliance on yourself, your efforts to obtain righteousness, your imagined merits and cast yourself at his feet like a pauper seeking a gift from a benefactor. Turn from going your own way and deliberately decide to yield your life to God and to righteousness. Make that U-turn and come to him through Christ. You may not yet know a lot of facts about him but if you put your trust in the Lord Jesus he will introduce you to God and bring you into a real personal relationship with him. You will come to know him.

An African boy was being taunted by his pals because he had never seen the chief or king of his tribe. He determined to make a long journey to the town in which the king lived. When he got there he found the king's palace and ventured up to the gate. A guard stopped him and would not let him go any further. He pleaded that he had come a long way and that he had spent all his money to make the journey but still he was not allowed in - there was no way he was going to see the king. He sat down by the wall, buried his head in his knees and began to cry. A big tall man in long flowing robes came along and asked what was wrong. 'I've made a long journey to come here because I want to see the king. I've spent all my money but the guard won't let me pass the gate of the king's house.'

'Give me your hand,' said the man and together they walked towards the gate. This time the guard sprung to attention, saluted the man and the boy and the two entered the king's palace. They walked through some corridors and eventually reached a room where the king was sitting. The man introduced the boy and told his story and the king kindly gave him a shining shilling (today's equivalent might be five pounds).

What was the secret that got that boy into the king's presence? It was that the tall man who gave him his hand was the king's son. He lived in the palace and the guard had no right to stop him going in to it. He led the boy to his father, the king. He introduced him to the king and the boy was able to go home and tell his friends that he had not only seen the king but had actually talked to him - he knew him!

That surely illustrates the role of the Lord Jesus - no one can come to the Father except through him. As the Son of God, he lives with his Father and he can take us into his Father's presence if we put our hand of faith into his strong hand of promise and let him bring us to God. He and he alone can bring us to God.

DON'T DELAY - REPENT and BELIEVE. Call on him - rest in him and be saved.

'If you seek him with all your heart, you will surely find him.'